Within everyone is an inner spark calling us toward a higher purpose. For some, that purpose is all about becoming a spiritual practitioner—using our mediumship, psychic, or healing abilities to help others and positively impact the world. This calling is impossible to ignore; a persistent pull that keeps showing up, time and time again. In this book, we'll dive into the journey of the spiritual practitioner and discover how to turn this calling into a rewarding, full-time spiritual business.

A Guide to Launching and Scaling Your Spiritual Practice
as a Psychic, Medium, or Healer

FULL-TIME SPIRITUAL BUSINESS

JOHAN POULSEN

Copyright © 2023
JOHAN POULSEN
FULL-TIME SPIRITUAL BUSINESS
A Guide to Launching and Scaling Your Spiritual Practice as a Psychic, Medium, or Healer

All Rights Reserved. No part of this book may be reproduced by any mechanical, photographic, or electronic process or in the form of a photographic recording; nor may it be stored in a retrieval system, transmitted, copied for public or private use, or otherwise —other than for "fair use" as brief quotations embodied in articles and reviews—without prior written permission of the publisher. The author of this book does not dispense financial or medical advice or prescribe the use of any techniques as a form of treatment for physical, emotional, or medical problems without the advice of a physician, either directly or indirectly. The author's intent is only to offer information of a general nature on how to grow your spiritual business and take the next step in your spiritual career. In the event that you use any of the information in this book for yourself, the author and the publisher assume no responsibility for your actions. To protect the privacy of others, certain names and details have been changed.

JOHAN POULSEN

Printed Worldwide
First Printing 2023
First Edition 2023

Hardcover ISBN: 978-91-988490-0-4
Paperback ISBN: 978-91-988490-1-1
E-book ISBN: 978-91-988490-2-8
Audiobook ISBN: 978-91-988490-3-5

Table of Contents

Introduction..1
Welcome..4
My goal for you..6
About me..8
Disclaimer...11
Chapter 1: Time to catch up!....................................13
    Let's talk about you...16
    Before we move on...18
Chapter 2: Our ideal customers.................................21
    Misconception #1..23
    The bubble..26
    Woo-woo...29
Chapter 3: Your personal brand.................................31
    Misconception #2..33
    What image do you present?.............................35
Chapter 4: Regular vs. spiritual business..................39
    Misconception #3..41
    A niche industry...44
Chapter 5: Full-time spiritual business......................47
    A different energy..49
    Our website...50
    Let's break it down...51
        Landing page..51

  Clarity..52
  It's not about you..............................52
  Your resume.......................................53
  Our services.......................................53
  Using the right language.................54
  URL & Email 55
Chapter 6: Social media and marketing....................57
 Your digital business card..........................59
 Let's break it down.......................................61
  Private vs. business............................61
  Being consistent..................................62
  Marketing strategy.............................63
  Ads targeting.......................................64
  Patience..65
Chapter 7: A complete experience.............................67
 Understanding the client's journey..................69
 Where do you meet your clients?.....................71
 Important information................................74
 Working in the same place..........................76
Chapter 8: Money and payment...............................79
 Money-challenges..81
 Should spirituality be free?.............................83
 Let's break it down..85
  How much do you need?....................85
  The importance of quality pricing..........86
  Hours per week....................................87
  It's all about the numbers.................88
  Comfortable pricing............................89
  No arguing..91
  Payment systems.................................92
Chapter 9: Automate your business............................95
 Identifying the roadblocks...........................99
 When our system works..............................101
 Only work when you work..........................103

- Chapter 10: Thinking outside the box 107
  - Services 110
  - Groups 112
  - Demonstrations (séances) 114
  - Courses 117
  - Fairs and events 119
    - Fairs 119
    - Events 121
  - Two more things 122
- Chapter 11: Working online 125
  - Services 127
  - Pros and cons 129
  - Online courses 132
  - Physical or digital products 134
  - The importance of quality 136
  - First step online 138
  - The big picture 140
- Chapter 12: Entrepreneurship 143
  - Why does this matter? 146
  - Being professional 148
- Chapter 13: Next step 151
  - The checklist 155
  - The end 156
- Checklist 158
  - Audience and clarity 158
  - Website essentials 158
  - Social media and marketing 159
  - The client experience 159
  - Money and payments 160
  - Automating 160
  - Thinking outside the box (diversifying services) .. 160
  - Business growth 161
- About the author 162

INTRODUCTION

Once upon a time, many years ago, I found myself at a spiritualist center in the charming seaside town of Paignton, on the south coast of England. I traveled there from Sweden with a few friends to attend a workshop, give readings, and get the chance to practice my mediumship demonstration skills in front of a British audience.

After years of reading books and studying on my own, I had finally found a mentor and a group of like-minded people to share my development journey with. This was no longer the odd interest I had kept hidden for so long, but rather a genuine calling I now shared with my new-found friends.

Right from the beginning, the entire trip felt like an incredible adventure. England and Paignton had a completely different perspective on mediumship. They were organized with centers, teachers, courses, and the world's largest organization connected to spiritualism—the SNU. What was considered pretty "woo-woo" back home in Sweden was a usual way of life in Paignton.

We spent the weekend participating in exercises, giving readings, and doing platform demonstrations for the local audience. We stayed at a cozy bed-and-breakfast, and in the evenings, we enjoyed dinner at the pub just around the corner. I had a fantastic time, and I will always cherish that weekend with warmth in my heart.

On the last day, I scheduled my own reading with one of the local British mediums. I've lost some important people in my life and wanted to see if they would come through. And, of course, I was always eager to study a professional medium at work. From the start, my mother came through, and the medium described her unforgettable (and unnecessarily large) 70s-style sunglasses. It was an emotional and moving reading that reminded me of the importance of our work as mediums and spiritual practitioners.

After the reading, I waited as the medium transferred the audio recording to a CD for me to keep. We chatted briefly about my experience over the weekend at the center, and then the medium said, "I can feel you really want to do this full-time." And yes, he was spot on. For the first time in my life, after trying around 30 different jobs, the idea of working full time with my mediumship felt like the exciting career I had always dreamed of. Helping people connect with their lost loved ones on the other side and passing on their healing messages was something I wanted to do full-time. But was it even possible? Could I make a living doing what I loved while supporting myself and my future family as a medium?

Fast forward about 14 years, and I can confidently tell you yes, it's possible. Anyone who feels called to work full-time as a spiritual practitioner can make this a reality. Mediumship, psychic abilities, and healing aren't just spiritual hobbies performed behind closed doors; they are in-demand services with a growing number of interested customers. However, the path to building a spiritual business differs from what many people might think. Staying in our spiritual bubble and offering our services to like-minded people in closed Facebook groups isn't enough. We need to learn how to "switch hats" and separate our personal spirituality from our spiritual business. Like any practitioner in any field, we must be professional to make it work. And in this book, I'll show you exactly how to do that.

Welcome

Hi! I'm Johan, and I want to welcome you on this journey toward building a full-time spiritual career. I'm excited to guide you through this book and help you either launch or scale your spiritual business.

Most people who follow the path of becoming spiritual practitioners usually recognize that inner spark or pull. You want to do something meaningful, something you're passionate about, and, above all, you feel called to help others through your spiritual gifts. But to do that, you need enough time and financial security to relax and focus on your clients. You need a functioning business that takes care of you while you care for others. And, unfortunately, that's easier said than done. As spiritually-minded people, we usually don't spend much time in the energy of business. We may be educated and knowledgeable in our area of expertise, we might know all about our clients' energy, auras, and chakras, but our spiritual skills don't apply when it comes to business.

So, what do we do? Well, usually one of two things happen: We build a basic website and put our Gmail on the first page. Then we post a discounted offer in a spiritual Facebook group and wait. Well, at least we gave it a try, and if we're lucky, we might be able to turn our spiritual abilities into a time-consuming hobby. Or, option number two, we don't even give our inner calling a fair chance, and we settle for the classic thought: "If this is meant to be, the universe will provide". Well, it is meant to be, but I'm sorry to say it's not the universe's job to provide us with a functioning business—it's our job. The universe will always nudge us in the right direction; however, it will never take away our opportunity to grow. And, in the grand scheme of things, this is good news.

If we look at the spiritual industry today, there's no shortage of information, books, courses, etc., connected to developing our spiritual skills. Whether you're a medium, psychic, or healer, there's an endless supply of resources. Anyone interested in developing their spiritual abilities can find a mentor or teacher with a quick Google search. But then what? What happens after we finish? What do we do with those diplomas we worked so hard for? How do we turn our passion into something we can do full-time? Well, we do what they do in all other industries: we study those who have gone before us.

My goal for you

This book aims to give you a deeper insight into what it means to run a successful spiritual business because it's not the same as "any other business". In offering spiritual services, we often face many questions from our clients. Unlike clients in other types of businesses, our clients often have subconscious questions based on their beliefs and feelings about what we do. As spiritual practitioners, it's not enough to just state facts and then list the benefits of what we do. No, the services we provide connect with our clients on a deeper level, and when we market and sell our sessions, readings, or products, we usually have only one tool at our disposal: trust. If our clients don't trust us, then we have no business. And to earn that trust and for clients to let us be their spiritual practitioners, we need to be professionals. And that, unfortunately, is an area where many spiritual practitioners fall short. If we can't build trust and provide our clients with a professional experience, creating a full-time spiritual career will be tough.

In the following chapters, I'll guide you step-by-step, showing you what to do or not when starting and scaling a spiritual business. This book is the result of many years of trial and error before I understood the subtle differences between our industry and others. This is the book I wish I could have read a long time ago, and by passing on this information, I hope you can avoid investing unnecessary time, energy, and money trying to figure this out on your own.

By the end of this book, you'll know how a spiritual business works. You'll learn to attract customers and clients and fill up your booking calendar. You'll know what clients expect from you and how to get paid adequately for your work. You'll learn how to build a stable foundation, so you won't have to worry about surviving financially. Most importantly, you'll discover your ideal customer (probably not who you think it is).

About Me

I believe many people embark on a spiritual journey due to wanted or unwanted changes in their lives. The path of a spiritual practitioner isn't something suggested by a parent or guidance counselor; it begins in the heart, often as a result of personal challenges. By overcoming these challenges and finding the strength to change, we end up wanting the same for others. Whether it's guidance, connecting with a loved one in spirit, or healing, our work as spiritual practitioners often stems from our transformative experiences.

My journey into mediumship began in a small village outside Stockholm, Sweden. I lost my mother when I was nine years old, which left me with many questions about life, death, and the afterlife. In my early teens, I discovered the concepts of mediumship and psychic abilities, and for years, I devoured every book I could find on the subject. As I grew older, my interest intensified, and by my late 20s, I had attended numerous trainings, courses, and workshops. Throughout these years, I also pursued various academic and professional paths, but a part of me always felt drawn toward my spiritual interests.

As I turned 30, it was time to take the leap and start doing mediumship "for real". As a student, I had been giving readings for years, but the idea of launching a professional mediumship business was daunting. However, after a serious talk with myself, I finally took the plunge. I designed a website to offer my services as a medium, created a new Facebook profile (to keep it a secret from my friends), and opened up my calendar for bookings.

Honestly, I had a pretty good start. Whether it was due to my location in Stockholm or my knowledge of ranking websites on Google, I began getting clients. I initially worked other jobs to supplement my income but eventually phased them out. Even though my calendar had gaps, I still felt like I was "working". However, at the end of my first year, my accountant's financial statement showed that my earnings were not what I had imagined. After factoring in taxes, office rent, and online service costs, I realized I probably would have been better off collecting empty soda cans. I worked six to seven days a week, doing readings and feeling busy, but my business was still struggling. My heart and focus were the same then as now: to help my clients in the best possible way. However, I didn't understand that my spirituality and my business were two separate things. I didn't realize the importance of a professional structure in which I could work on my terms, earn a living, and still provide heartfelt services to my clients.

It's been 14 years now since I started giving professional readings. I have worked fulltime as a medium for many years, offering private readings, group sessions, stage demonstrations, courses, private tutoring, circles, workshops, and events. I have discussed mediumship in interviews and magazines, and through the TV show

Swedish Mediums, Warner Bros. gave me the opportunity to present my work to a larger audience. I have authored a book— *Modern Mediumship: A Complete (Woo-Woo-Free) Course to Become a Successful Psychic Medium*— and run an online course platform that, as of this writing, has helped over 1,400 people develop their mediumship.

Today, I have figured out how to make it work. I'm not everywhere all the time, and I can afford to say no when something doesn't feel right or fit my schedule. I work with clients and students whom I feel I can genuinely help, and my business supports a family of four. Thanks to a professional structure that allows me to switch between working with clients and working on my business, I now work fewer hours but achieve and earn more than before. I share this not to boast about my accomplishments, but because I know that you can make it work too.

Disclaimer

The information presented in this book is based on my personal experience and the strategies I've employed to build my own spiritual business, keep my calendar booked, and maintain a steady flow of new customers and clients. My goal has never been to accumulate excess wealth; as long as I can do the work I love and create a financially secure and stress-free life for myself and my family, I consider my business successful.

Running a spiritual business, or any business for that matter, requires you to actively "run it". You need to be proactive and consistently strive to grow your business. However, not everyone translates the knowledge they acquire from books into action. I need to be clear on this point: I can provide you with the knowledge and information you need to start and grow your spiritual business, but it's up to you to take action. I can't do the work for you or guarantee specific results. These strategies have worked well for me over the years, and if you apply what you learn in this book, you should also see results.

With that said, the information in this book should be regarded as suggestions rather than definitive solutions, and, of course, I'm not giving financial advice. Take what works for you and leave the rest. These strategies and ideas are based on my experience working in the Swedish market, and although these concepts are fairly universal, there may be differences in their application depending on your country. If you need specific, technical, or legal advice related to business, finance, or marketing, consult a licensed professional in those respective fields.

CHAPTER 1
TIME TO CATCH UP!

Let's start this chapter with a couple of questions: Are there any differences between a spiritual business and other types of businesses? Is there a distinction between being a medium, psychic, or healer compared to, for example, a hairdresser or massage therapist?

The answer is YES; there is a significant difference! One notable aspect is that the spiritual field has not quite "kept up" or "caught up" with other industries. For instance, there's still a certain taboo associated with money or the marketing of spiritual services, which isn't as common in other sectors. I often see people with strong opinions about the pricing of our services, and it's not unusual for these to come from within our own spiritual community, even from fellow practitioners. This leads to many mediums, psychics, and healers, who may have invested everything to work full-time in their field, now living just on or below the threshold of financial sustainability.

Another factor that affects all types of spiritual businesses is the long-standing "old image" associated with our work. It may sound strange, but many people still envision a medium as an "old fortune teller in a dark basement". Even though we, as practitioners, have a more modern view of our work, this outdated image sometimes misleads or scares our clients. Instead of clients embracing the experience of our services, we often still have to deal with age-old questions like, "Is this real or not?" All of this affects the confidence of new mediums, psychics, and healers, causing many to feel uncomfortable being open about their work. They shy away from revealing their spiritual side and avoid using their real names or pictures on websites and social media. Ultimately, this leads to spiritual practitioners not being perceived as professionals, which impacts our opportunities to run serious and functional businesses.

Over the last couple of years, the interest in spirituality has grown rapidly, and today there is a HUGE demand for spiritual services. There are more potential clients than practitioners available to meet their needs, and many could easily work full-time in their spiritual business. But to achieve that, to evolve and "catch up" with other industries, we must offer the world, especially our clients, a "new image". We need to stand up for what we do, be open about who we are, and demonstrate that we are as professional as any other industry. If we can do that, we'll no longer have to work multiple jobs to afford to express our spiritual calling

Let's talk about you

Where are you on your journey as a spiritual practitioner? I imagine you've been interested in this field for quite some time. You've probably taken courses and invested both time and money into developing the abilities you want to work with today. At some point, you might have asked yourself, "Could I earn extra income from my spiritual work or even do this full-time?" Or perhaps you feel as I did: "This is my thing. This is what I was born to do, and I just have to make it work!"

Regardless of the scale at which you want to do this—whether it's for extra income, parttime, or full-time—you'll face the same challenges and go through the same phases as all spiritual practitioners. I usually describe this in three steps: "Student" on one end, "professional" on the other, and in the middle, where many practitioners find themselves today, is "frustration". You may have invested a lot of time and energy trying to make it work. You're active on social media, maybe putting together small events, and doing everything to launch and establish your own business. The more time you invest, the more often you grapple with the thought, "Will I make it? Is it worth it?" I know this doesn't apply to everyone. Most people who get into this field do so gradually while still maintaining the security of a regular job, but overcoming this step and transitioning into a full-time spiritual business is the same for everyone. If you want to do this on a larger scale, there will come a day when uncertainty creeps in and you realize you're somewhere in the middle, in the "frustration" phase.

The foundation of a functioning spiritual business lies in working with clients, primarily through private sessions: readings, healings, or any other services you offer. To build a spiritual business, the "base" of the business (at least initially) must be built on hourly sessions. Once you have everything up and running and have gained a reputation over time, you can switch this "base" for something else. For instance, many well-known and established mediums travel around, building their businesses by only doing large-scale stage demonstrations. However, to attract a larger audience and make a living from these types of demonstrations, you must first establish yourself by working with many clients, and this is done through private sessions. So, we can agree that to do many private sessions and build up this base or foundation in our business, we need customers and clients to book our services. If no one books, nothing happens.

Before we move on

Two things to keep in mind before we continue to the next chapter: First, try to maintain an open mind and reflect on the information presented in this book. What we discuss here is not merely "my opinions" about spiritual business but the experiences and facts drawn from working with thousands of clients over many years. While there may be aspects of our industry we wish functioned differently, our opinions about how things "should" work won't help us build a successful business. Instead, we need to focus on the strategies that are proven to work and implement them in our own practice.

Second, it's essential to distinguish between "practice" and "business" in all types of ventures, especially spiritual ones, as well as crucial to keep these two components separate. This book will primarily address the "business" aspect. Many spiritual practitioners can become a bit stuck in the energy and desire to help their clients, which is a good thing. After all, that's our job. However, you can't solely focus on this energy if you aim to establish a thriving business. When you're not working directly with clients, you need to "switch hats" and be comfortable with marketing, setting appropriate fees, and handling other business-related tasks.

From here on, we'll discuss strategies and techniques to attract more customers and increase your income. It's important to be open to these ideas. If you still adhere to the "old picture" that spiritual abilities are a "special gift you got for free" and should not be charged for, this book might not be the right fit for you. However, if you're interested in building a successful business that allows you to do what you love and help as many clients as possible, then let's move forward.

CHAPTER 2
OUR IDEAL CUSTOMERS

Before diving into the important steps to make our spiritual business thrive, we must first address three common misconceptions that often hold practitioners back. In this chapter, we will look at the first one, connected to our ideal customers. Understanding these misconceptions is crucial to avoiding turning our business into just a "spiritual hobby", where a lot of time and effort results in nothing.

As I mentioned earlier, our primary goal for a spiritual business is to build a solid foundation, or "base"—a calendar filled with bookings, providing us with consistent work. When we have that, we can then create and offer various courses, events, and anything else we desire. However, to build this base, we must first identify and connect with our ideal customers, those most likely to book private sessions, readings, or healing.

MISCONCEPTION #1

As a medium, psychic, healer, or any other spiritual practitioner, who is our ideal customer? Who needs our services the most and can form the base of our business? And, when I talk about the "base" of our business, I'm referring to new customers rather than regular, recurring ones. It's important to note that spiritual services, particularly mediumship and psychic readings, can become addictive for some clients, causing them to lose the ability to make their own life decisions. That's why I see 95% of my clients only once. When working as mediums or psychics, we don't want to "learn to know" our clients; that will affect our readings. As healers, this is not an issue, and working with recurring customers is ok.

So, if I were to ask, "Who are our ideal customers?" there is a big chance many practitioners would answer, "Our ideal customers are spiritually interested people!" Unfortunately, that's not necessarily true. Surprisingly, many clients seeking mediums, psychics, and healers are only moderately or not spiritually interested. Though it may seem counterintuitive, the reality is that most people who are actually willing to book and pay for a reading or healing session don't belong to our spiritual community, or "bubble", and have little interest in the philosophy behind our work. Of course, there are exceptions, but the largest pool of potential clients comes from a specific target group with moderate or no spiritual interest.

To give you an example: Many people get married and have their children baptized in a church, but only a small fraction of them are actually active within the church. They go there when they have a specific need, like a wedding, baptism, or funeral. Beyond that, they spend little to no time or energy on the belief system associated with the church (note that this example is just to illustrate a behavior, not to discuss faith or religion). Similarly, people seek out mediums, healers, and other spiritual practitioners because they currently have a "need" for what we offer, but unlike us, they don't feel the urge to be part of our spiritual world or "bubble".

Throughout this book, I'll frequently refer to the term "spiritual bubble". The bubble represents those of us who actively practice or have an ongoing interest in spiritual matters. We are "inside the spiritual bubble", while people who are moderately interested or not interested are "outside the bubble". And these people outside the bubble form the base and foundation we need for a successful spiritual business.

Now, you might be wondering, "Can this really be true? It seems counterintuitive." You'd expect that we'd provide spiritual services to those who are actively interested in spirituality. While that seems logical, the reality is different. If we offer courses, make TV appearances, or even write books, we sell "spirituality" to customers inside the bubble. But when it comes to private sessions, which should be the base of our business, we don't sell spirituality.

Instead, what our customers outside the bubble are looking for is "information" or something related to "health" rather than spirituality. People consult mediums to connect with a loved one on the other side (information) or to seek answers to life's questions (also information). Others approach healers to find balance or improve their health. A majority of the clients I've had over the years have been "regular people", outside the bubble, who were openly skeptical and disinterested in my spirituality. However, they needed to contact a loved one or get information, which is how I've been able to help them and build a base in my business.

If you work with private readings or other hour-based services and consistently have a fully booked calendar, you'll find that 90% of your clients will most likely be women between the ages of 45 and 60. They will typically have a moderate or even no interest in spirituality, and there's a high chance they work in healthcare or care for others in some capacity. This isn't a made-up scenario; it's based on 14 years of experience and thousands of private readings.

It's important to note that these statistics are primarily based on mediumship and psychic readings. Although I have a background in various healing methods, my experience in that area is not as extensive. However, the healing work I have done over the years suggests that clients seeking those services fall into the same demographic, which may also apply to other forms of spiritual practice when offered as private sessions.

The bubble

Now that we know who our ideal clients are, how can we utilize this information effectively? One example I see almost daily is mediums, psychics, and healers advertising their services on social media, especially within Facebook groups. It's great to see people actively trying to reach new clients. However, there's a problem. These "spiritual groups" mostly attract spiritually interested people, just like you and me. While there's nothing wrong with these groups (I'm a member of several myself), we must remember the concept of "the bubble". These spiritual groups embody the bubble, and their active members are "inside the bubble". These groups, consisting of people like us with a high spiritual interest, are too small to sustain a spiritual business or practice. By only being visible in these groups, we fail to reach the types of people most likely to book our services.

Imagine a Facebook group with about 10,000 members. Around 2-3,000 people in this group may be spiritual practitioners offering services. Another 2-3,000 people might have taken courses and made some progress in their spiritual development. The remaining 3-4,000 people are likely to be very interested but haven't taken any active steps yet to develop their spiritual abilities. In this environment, all mediums, psychics, healers, and other practitioners are competing to promote their services to people who are already well-informed and may not have a pressing need for a reading or healing session. These individuals are part of the group due to their spiritual interests, and even though they might occasionally buy a $10 tarot reading, there is not a big "need" there.

People who are very interested in what we do have likely already visited various mediums and healers, and they may even have a "favorite medium" they visit once a year. So, a Facebook group that appears to be the "right place" to advertise your services may actually be a rather cold marketplace from a business perspective. To clarify, let's consider another example: Imagine you're a hairdresser in a Facebook group for hairdressers, and you try to advertise your services there. How does that sound? Hairdressers don't market to other hairdressers because there's no demand; if a hairdresser wants a haircut, they can get it for free at work from a colleague. So, there's no reason to advertise "haircut and blowdry" to another hairdresser, as they are part of the same "bubble". Hairdressers, therefore, market their products and services to customers outside of their bubble.

Returning to our example of spiritual Facebook groups, the members of these groups already have their needs met. They see 20-30 different types of readings offered daily in their Facebook feed, and should they ever need these services, they already have their favorite practitioner outside the group. The mediums, psychics, and healers in the group have valuable, high-quality services that would be perfect if they reached the right customers.

However, these services are marketed to people "interested in spirituality" instead of those with a "need" for what we offer. So the practitioners keep lowering their prices, thinking the problem is their offer.

Someone who has lost a loved one or is facing a critical life decision doesn't automatically become "spiritually interested" and start joining every spiritual Facebook group. However, they do have a "need" for what we offer, and these clients are the ones most likely to book our services, but only if they can find us and get a professional impression of who we are and what we do.

Woo-woo

Before we move on to the next chapter and misconception #2, we'll introduce a term or phrase that we'll use as a measurement throughout this book. This phrase is quite common within the field of spirituality, and many people actually use it as a positive expression in their spiritual marketing. I use it as a tool when coaching private students on their websites, texts, social media, etc., when they're about to start their businesses.

And what we're discussing here is the term "woo-woo". This phrase is an excellent and effective way to describe and clarify the difference between our world "inside the bubble" and the experiences of potential clients who aren't familiar with what we do. Often, the difference between a customer choosing to book a session or not comes down to the degree of "woo-woo" we, as practitioners, project.

Let's consider a hypothetical example: Say your car has a problem and needs to be fixed. You search Google for a local car repair shop and find a website that says, "Steve's Car Repair; we fix your car." Perfect, that'll do the trick. But now imagine if it said, "Steve's Car Repair; we fix your car using the BT17 method." Wait, what? What does that mean? Is the BT17 method good or bad? Do I need to research this? No, I'll find another repair shop instead to avoid this BT17 thing I don't understand.

Just like our spiritual bubble, all industries have their own "bubble" of people who are very knowledgeable within their field or work. In this example, Steve's Car Repair shifts from targeting everyone who needs car repairs to suddenly marketing to a much smaller and narrower group of customers by diving into their bubble. The BT17 method might be fantastic, but for those of us who don't know what it is, it's a bit too unclear, so we back off and find a "normal" repair shop instead.

You, I, and those who work within our bubble know that there's nothing woo-woo about what we do (from a negative perspective). But there's a fine line for our target customers—the ones we need to build our base and business on. If something feels strange, unusual, or just too "woo-woo", there's a high chance we'll lose them as customers. So, it's crucial to remember this important distinction: if we're offering courses, stage performances, writing books, or doing TV appearances, we're selling "spirituality" to people "inside the bubble". However, our private sessions, which we need to form the base and foundation of our business, cater to people outside the bubble. And for them, too much woo-woo can be perceived negatively.

CHAPTER 3
YOUR PERSONAL BRAND

In this chapter, we'll discuss the second common misconception in the spiritual business world, which is related to you, your personal brand, and how potential clients perceive you. Remember that when I mention "marketing" yourself, I'm not just referring to active advertising; it encompasses everything from your website to individual social media posts. Essentially, every time you are visible to potential clients, it counts as marketing.

MISCONCEPTION #2

As spiritual practitioners and business owners, we sometimes make the mistake of focusing too much on "what we do". It's easy to see why this seems logical: isn't it obvious that our clients are interested in our services? While this is true, before clients become interested in booking your services, they'll first be drawn to "who you are". Initial contact with new customers or clients is always based on your persona.

It's important to remember that regardless of the services we provide—be it mediumship, psychic readings, healing, or anything else—these experiences can be incredibly personal and private for our clients. Seeking someone who can "read" their innermost feelings or work with their energy is an intimate experience. Therefore, no matter what services or prices you offer, clients will want to "check you out" before booking a session.

This is where the concept of "woo-woo" comes in. Clients will book a session with you because YOU are YOU. If you project an overly spiritual or mystical image, you'll only attract clients within that narrow niche, and the number of potential clients won't be enough to sustain a business. However, if you present a professional and open image, the right customer group will feel comfortable with you and book your services.

When I use terms like "woo-woo" or "overly spiritual", I don't mean anything negative. I mention them to highlight the difference between our world inside the spiritual bubble and the perception potential customers have of what we do and who we are. It's important to be authentic and true to yourself, but it's equally crucial to understand the image you're projecting. If your business isn't growing, it's not because there are no customers—there are plenty. The issue is more likely the image you present to potential clients.

As a quick side note, don't compare your marketing to that of well-known or established mediums or healers. Some individuals, due to their media exposure, can sustain their businesses entirely within the "spiritual bubble". They don't need to worry about being perceived as too "woo-woo" since most of their customers have a high level of spiritual interest. Often, these famous individuals reduce or stop offering private sessions and instead focus on performances, TV appearances, and writing books. This approach works well for those who are already established in the spiritual field. However, for those starting a new spiritual business or trying to grow an existing one, it's vital to remember that your client base must be built outside the bubble, and the impression you create and the image you project become crucial.

What image do you present?

As a spiritual practitioner, what image do you present to your customers? This may, of course, differ depending on how long you've been in the business. If you're new to the field and just starting to work with clients, perhaps you haven't yet established an image or "brand" for yourself. You haven't started marketing yourself. Regardless of whether you're a newcomer or a seasoned practitioner, this aspect is essential.

Using my services and courses as an example, about 99% of my clients or students have already formed an opinion of me before becoming customers. They may have visited my website, read my books, or seen my social media posts, blogs, podcasts, or TV appearances. They have already created an image and perception of who I am as a person. That image (hopefully) resonated with them, leading them to choose me as their spiritual practitioner.

My point is that no matter how much time, planning, and energy I invest in my mediumship, business, or courses, it won't matter if I don't give my potential students and clients a chance to know me. The image I present is hundred percent authentic, and all of this information is readily available on my websites, Facebook, Instagram, and podcasts, where I share personal aspects of my life. By being open, transparent, and honest about who I am, my clients and students can feel secure when they decide to invest their time and money in my services.

Let's examine the image you present to potential clients. As I mentioned earlier, if you have just started working with clients, you may not have developed your personal brand yet. However, this information can still be valuable for your journey. Suppose you make a post in a Facebook group offering something like, "Angel card reading for 30 minutes, $20". If I see this post and think, "Yes, that's something I'd like to try," how can I get an idea of who you are and feel confident that you're the right person for this card reading? What information do you provide to help me get to know you? For instance, what name do you use on social media? Is it your name, for example, "Anna Smith Medium" or something made up like "Medium Nana"? What image do you have on your Facebook page? A clear and friendly picture of your face or a psychedelic chakra image? Is there a link to a website where I can learn more about you and your approach to spirituality? How can I determine whether you're just right or too "woo-woo" for my taste?

I want to emphasize the importance of giving your customers an honest image of who you are. This is an issue in our industry, especially among new spiritual practitioners. I often see mediums, healers, and other spiritual practitioners attempting to offer services while remaining entirely anonymous, trying to sell something without revealing their identity. I'm unaware of any other industry where clients are expected to pay for a service or product without knowing from whom they're purchasing. It might sound logical, but if you've been in the spiritual bubble for a while and are a member of spiritual Facebook groups, you know exactly what I mean. There are variations of this, such as using a made-up name like "Moon Star" with a highly spiritual profile picture or a modified name like "Medium Nana" and a photo taken slightly from behind, hiding the face.

If you want to grow your spiritual business, whether for extra income or as a full-time career, you MUST be comfortable being open about who you are. Remember, your target customers are people outside the spiritual bubble who want to feel secure when seeking answers, contact, or healing from you. They can't overcome the "woo-woo threshold" if they don't know who you are or what you look like. To have a successful business with a steady flow of clients, you must be transparent about your identity. What we offer is something positive, loving, and beneficial. Be proud of it and stand up for your beliefs. There will always be people with opinions about our work, but that's their issue. People have opinions about everything, and we can't let them stop us from doing our job. If clients can get an honest and warm impression of who we are, they will be more likely to purchase our services.

CHAPTER 4
REGULAR VS SPIRITUAL BUSINESS

In this chapter, we'll tackle misconception #3, which addresses the difference between a "regular" and a spiritual business. We touched on this in chapter one, but we first needed to cover misconception #1—"understanding who our ideal customers are"—before diving deeper into this topic. We previously used the example of a hairdresser, and we will do so again to illustrate this difference. Remember, always focus on the right customer group—those outside the spiritual "bubble" who require our services and are a large enough group to support a viable business.

MISCONCEPTION #3

Imagine that you need a haircut. You book an appointment with a hairdresser; you go there and get your hair cut. Simple, right? It's straightforward because you know what to expect. You've had haircuts before, and the whole process feels natural. There are no questions.

Now, picture one of our clients—someone who needs our spiritual services but is "outside the bubble" and unfamiliar with spiritual matters. For this person, a private reading or healing session may be unlike anything they've ever experienced. They're unsure of what to expect and how it works, and they may even be uncertain about their thoughts or beliefs regarding our services. This is where the distinction lies between a regular and a spiritual business. When customers know what to expect, it's easy for them to make a decision and book an appointment, like with a hairdresser. Even if you've never been to a hairdresser, you know what happens there—your hair gets cut. But with our services, such as mediumship, healing, or other spiritual practices, most customers and clients don't have a clear idea of what we do or how it works.

They may have an idea of the concept, but many haven't experienced spiritual services firsthand.

Anything that raises questions creates a barrier between the client and us. If they feel uncertain about what they're getting into, they may hesitate and avoid booking an appointment. It's essential to understand this point. We must differentiate between our own clear perception of what we do and adjust our image and marketing to ensure the right customer group can understand and feel at ease booking our services.

So, how do we bridge the gap between a regular and a spiritual business? First, we need to be clear and transparent about what we do. Second, we need to anticipate our clients' questions and concerns. As mediums, psychics, and healers, our way of working is often slightly automatic, a process we don't think about at the moment. We just do it. For us, all of this is normal and natural, and we focus on the results, not on how we get there. But remember that everything we do is an internal process that our clients may not understand. This lack of understanding can lead to questions and hesitation when booking our services. Therefore, our job is to give our clients a clear idea of what to expect when booking and attending a reading or healing session. And here are the first basic steps to achieve this:

1. We need to have a website that shows who we are and explains our services in understandable terms so clients know what to expect without getting lost in spiritual details.

2. Always include a picture of ourselves and, if possible, the room where we conduct our sessions. How does the room look? Is it nice and inviting?

3. Explain how we work: for instance, "I use tarot or angel cards", or "During a healing session, you'll sit or lie down", "I won't touch you", or "I'll gently place my hands on your shoulders", depending on your approach.

4. Provide essential information like prices, address, whether clients should arrive early, wait outside, or knock on the door, payment options, and recording policies for readings. Do you record your readings? Should they do it? Or don't you allow it?

The clearer you are when providing information and answers in advance, the more clients you'll attract. You don't need to describe your entire "inner spiritual process", but giving your clients a sense of what will happen during their session is crucial.

Consider the example of a doctor performing a minor procedure or surgery. They carefully walk you through what will happen without detailing their personal or specific techniques. They focus on your experience, helping you feel calm and secure. The same principle applies to us as spiritual practitioners. We must eliminate as many questions and uncertainties as possible so that our clients feel at ease. Remember, unanswered questions will lead to clients backing out, resulting in fewer bookings.

A NICHE INDUSTRY

In today's business climate, almost all industries are focusing on niching down their services. Companies specialize in specific areas to cater to a particular customer group with specific needs. For example, in the past, you would go to a car repair shop for any issue with your car. Now, you have the choice of going to a tire shop, body shop, or general car repair shop. This is an example of how companies "niche" themselves to capture a particular group of customers. Regarding our spiritual services, one might think that being unique or offering a service that no one else has (or giving it a unique name) will guarantee more bookings. Naming a private session "24th Dimension Soul Reading", for example, might seem like it would help you stand out and attract clients. However, this approach can backfire.

Remember that we, as spiritual practitioners, already work in a highly "niche" industry. Our challenge isn't being unique; we're already super unique. We don't need to niche down further. Instead, we should aim to open up to a broader group of people, become more accessible and professional, and limit the "woo-woo" aspects.

Remember, our target customers are those outside the spiritual bubble. These are the people we need to form the base of our business. They know what happens at, for example, a car repair shop and can accept that industry's niching down. However, when it comes to spiritual services, they may not have a clear understanding of what we do. As practitioners, we should avoid making things more confusing by niching down more with services that only a few people understand. Established terms like "medium", "psychic", or "healer" are familiar enough for clients to accept and book a session. Going beyond this with terms like "24th Dimension Soul Reading" or "Healing with Violet Flame" can drive away customers.

This doesn't mean you should stop doing what you do. If you use the violet flame for healing, keep doing it. Just ensure that you and your business image are open, uncomplicated, and accessible. After a reading or session, when the client has gone through the experience, they might ask more specific questions about how it works. At that point, you can be as niche as you want since their uncertainty is gone.

The main focus here is lowering the barrier before a client books a session, ensuring you have enough customers for a successful business. Regardless of your methods or training, remember that your customers aren't as familiar with these topics as you are. Always communicate your image, business, and services clearly and simply to attract more clients.

CHAPTER 5
FULL-TIME SPIRITUAL BUSINESS

Now it's time to take what we've learned in the previous chapters and apply it in practice to shape our business, target the right customer group, and overcome the uncertainties that many clients face. In the next seven chapters, we'll examine various aspects of the business, learning how to market ourselves, attract customers, and provide a complete experience. Keep in mind that we're discussing strategy here, not spiritual practice—we're focusing entirely on the business aspect, securing a consistent flow of new clients, and increasing bookings in our calendar.

A DIFFERENT ENERGY

Our "spiritual business" differs from our "spiritual work". It involves an entirely different energy and mindset. When working with clients, we're used to being in our spiritual energy. But now, we must shift our energy and think differently: "How do I get customers to book my services?" For some practitioners, this can be challenging. Marketing ourselves may feel uncomfortable or inconsistent with our spiritual nature. It might seem a bit pushy, and it's easy to shy away and think, "If it's meant to be, it will happen by itself. I won't actively do anything— I'll just wait and hope customers find me on their own." However, know that there is nothing wrong with marketing yourself and reaching out with your services. Remember, many clients out there are searching for precisely what you offer. By embracing this entrepreneurial energy, we simply ensure that we present the best possible image of ourselves and our business, allowing customers to find us and feel confident in booking our services.

Our website

First, let's talk about our website. If you're new to your spiritual practice or just starting your business, you might not have a website yet, and that's okay. In that case, you have an excellent opportunity to get some pointers on how to approach this. If you already have a website, you can use it as a reference for what we'll discuss here.

Is a website necessary? Absolutely! Some practitioners believe that they can manage with just a Facebook page for now, but unfortunately, that's not enough. Your Facebook page markets your brand, while your website markets your services. Facebook or Instagram act as your "business card", while your website is your "storefront" that turns interested customers into revenue.

LET'S BREAK IT DOWN

What do we need to consider for our website? As always, we need to think about clients who belong to the "right customer group"—people who need our services but aren't fully informed about what we do, those outside our spiritual bubble. A website consists of text and images, but using the right text and images is crucial. Just because you have a website doesn't mean it's effective—it could be quite the opposite. So let's break it down into a few steps:

1. Landing page

The website's landing page (the first page your customers see when they click on a link from Facebook or find you on Google) should feature your photo, name, and what you do. For example, "Medium Anna Smith", along with a nice picture. Your potential clients, the right customer group, have come here because they want to know more about you. Booking your services comes later. At this point, they want to know if you "feel right" to them. Keep the first page relatively clean. Don't put all the information here; instead, have tabs at the top where customers can choose whether they want to read more about you, your services, or contact you.

2. Clarity

Clarity is essential for all pages, pictures, and texts on your website. Your images and texts convey a lot about who you are, and if you make it too complicated or too "woo-woo", many potential customers will leave the page and look for someone else. Remember, you don't need to describe your entire spiritual journey; you just need to provide a nice picture of who you are.

3. It's not about you

Avoid making the website "about you". This might sound odd because, of course, your website is about you, right? What I mean is that the text and information on your website can have different angles. Instead of emphasizing "your own spiritual journey", focus on "what you can do for your clients". So, even if you have texts describing your personal spiritual experiences, try to incorporate the angle of "how all of this will benefit your clients." For example, "This is me and my spiritual journey," and because of this, "my main goal became to help my clients with..." whatever it may be.

If you've ever been to view a new house or apartment, you know that the real estate agent always focuses on the property in relation to you and your needs. It's the same for us and our website: how can we best focus on the customer and meet their needs?

4. Your resume

This is something I mentioned in my first book, Modern Mediumship. If you've read it, you'll recognize some of these points, but it's worth emphasizing the importance (or unimportance) of your CV or resume. There's a slight misconception about qualifications on our website. Many people list their entire resume on their website, thinking it increases their credibility as practitioners. But unfortunately, it doesn't. An example of this could be: "Hi, I'm a medium, healer, therapist, nutritionist, corporate lawyer, marathon runner, and mother of five." All of this is great, and kudos to anyone who has accomplished all those things. But for our clients, this is not always perceived as something positive. When booking a session or a reading with, for example, a medium, they want someone who is dedicated, someone who has "always just been a medium". You and I, who are in "the bubble", know that it doesn't matter. You can be a lawyer and a great medium. But for our clients, who are not as familiar with this, a long resume can dilute your role as a medium. The thought in the client's mind becomes: "If this person went to law school, trained for marathons, and has five children, how much time have they actually spent working as a medium?" So, if we have a website that offers services as a medium, we should present ourselves based on our role as a medium and leave out the rest.

5. Our services

Let's look at our services, meaning what we actually sell on our website: psychic or mediumship readings, healing, tarot, palmistry, or anything else. The first important thing here, which relates to the previous point about our "resume", is that we need to be focused and clear about what we are: medium, psychic, healer, or something else. We also need to be equally focused on our services. We must clearly describe what we do so that clients outside our spiritual bubble can understand what they're getting into. Our services should also be fairly "linked" to each other, meaning they need to "fit together" as variations of the same core service. If our services are completely different from each other, we risk coming across as a "Jack of all trades, master of none".

In general, you shouldn't have more than three services on your website, which should be clearly linked to each other. For example, Private Healing Sessions, Group Healing, and Distance Healing. These are three variations of the same core service. Or, for example, Mediumship Reading, Mediumship Development Circle, and Stage Demonstrations. These are also three services that are linked to each other. We want to avoid psychic readings, therapy, and Nutritional Counseling. These are not linked, and for clients, this signals that the practitioner has scattered energy and isn't specialized in one specific field. And remember what we talked about earlier: we don't need to "niche down" like in other industries, but we do need to "stay in our niche". If someone is looking for a medium and visits our website, they expect us to offer mediumship services. If we offer other things, they will back away.

6. Using the right language

Use words and terminology that are established in our industry, terms that people outside the bubble understand and recognize, such as "medium", "healer", "psychic", or similar. If you invent new names and titles for what you do, such as "chakra counselor", you will lose customers. Very few people will book a session if they don't understand what you do.

7. URL & Email

The final point on this list is related to your contact information and your domain name. A domain name is the web address (URL) linked to your website, for example, www.annasmithmedium.com, and if you have this website with this address, your email address should be contact (or info) @annasmithmedium.com. Everything should be connected. What you should avoid, for several reasons, is having a website address (domain name) that isn't linked to you or what you do, for example, www.eternalmoonbeam.com, and then an email address on the website named nana61937@hotmail.com. Avoid doing that.

Having a proper web address and correct email address affects your business in several ways: First, it looks professional. Second, it makes it easier for people to find you when they search "mediums" on Google. Lastly, it shows your customers that you are serious and open about what you do. It's not more difficult to get a good web address and an email address than to get a bad one. When you create your first website, you will have it hosted by one of the many website providers. You pay a monthly fee, which can vary, but you can have a professional website for about $5-10 per month (don't go with a "free website"—an option that displays random ads on your site). With this subscription, you get to choose the website's "web address" and then an email address linked to your website. You can then log in to your website, make changes, see all your emails, etc.

Creating a website today is not too difficult, and most providers offer ready-made, attractive templates that you simply paste in your text and images. If your website provider offers ready-made templates, search in the category "coaching". Those templates are usually personal brand templates and are easily converted to a spiritual services website.

CHAPTER 6
SOCIAL MEDIA AND MARKETING

In this chapter, we're going to discuss social media and marketing, which tie in closely with the topic of our previous chapter, websites. Nowadays, most people are connected to some form of social media, such as Facebook, Instagram, Twitter, and many more. We've all become quite used to seeing advertisements on these platforms on a daily basis. However, like with everything else in life, there are different ways to approach social media and marketing, with specific best practices to follow. Simply having a presence on social media doesn't guarantee more customers.

Your digital business card

Let's build on what we have previously discussed, but this time focusing on social media. Our Facebook page (or whichever platform you prefer) is connected to our brand, representing "who we are", and everything we do on Facebook helps market us as individuals and spiritual practitioners. A common mistake I often see is people advertising their services and prices through Facebook posts, hoping to attract more clients. Social media acts as your "digital business card", allowing potential clients to form an initial impression of who you are. If you constantly approach them with an "offer" or a "price" before they even know you, it won't be very appealing

Imagine walking into a department store, and before you can even look around, a staff member approaches you holding a pair of pants, saying, "These cost $100." It feels strange, pushy, and off-putting. You'd prefer to browse, find something interesting, and then, when you're ready, know the price of the item you're considering. The same principle applies to our spiritual services. If you want to spark interest in yourself and your services, then direct clients to your website for more information, pricing, and booking options. If customers choose to click on a link in your Facebook post and read more on your website, they won't be taken aback by an offer or price details. However, if they're confronted with a Facebook post simply stating "healing $50", it can feel like things are going a bit too fast.

LET'S BREAK IT DOWN

In the last chapter, we discussed building a website to sell your services, and now we'll dive into using social media to market yourself and your brand. We'll focus on Facebook for now since it's currently the top platform for reaching our target audience (in 2023). However, social media is constantly evolving, so you might find another platform more suitable in the future. Regardless of your chosen platform, the basic principles we discuss here will still apply.

1. Private vs. Business

When it comes to Facebook, it's essential to understand the difference between a private and a business profile. Most users start with a private profile, which is created when they first join Facebook. But a private profile won't let you market your posts. To do that, you'll need to create a "page", which serves as a business or professional profile. Creating a page is easy and similar to creating a Facebook group. With a page, you can promote your posts (I'll explain how later), and it helps you separate your personal and professional lives. For example, you don't want customers to see photos from your grandma's 90th birthday. Your friends should connect with your private profile, while customers or followers should engage with your professional page. It's all managed within the same Facebook account, so there's no need to log in and out.

2. Being consistent

When you post on your professional Facebook page, you remind your followers (and potential customers) that you exist. If you don't have many followers yet, don't worry; you'll gain more as you start advertising your services. People will see what you do, become interested, and start following you to learn more. Eventually, they might book your services. Just remember to strike a balance and be mindful of your target audience. These people need your services but want to know you better before booking. Your task on Facebook or any other social media platform is to present yourself as a friendly and approachable spiritual practitioner. Make posts related to your work, like "Lovely day with healing clients" or "Getting ready for readings in an hour". These posts show who you are and what you do without being overly promotional. When it comes to selling private sessions, take a subtle approach. For example: "I've just opened up new dates for readings; check out the calendar on the website", and then include the link. This way, customers can choose if they want to know more.

3. Marketing strategy

When I mention marketing, you might think of newspaper ads, but it's not quite the same. Marketing on Facebook means paying to get your posts seen by more people. These posts don't need to have an offer or a price; their purpose is to promote you as a person. When clients are ready to book a reading, healing, or something else, your name will be at the back of their minds. Promoting a post can cost as little as $1-5 or more, so you can make progress on Facebook even with a tight budget.

Here's a strategy for promoting a Facebook post: First, create a regular post on your professional Facebook page with an appealing image, and include a short, friendly text about what's happening in your business (make sure it's clear what you do: medium, healer, etc.). Add a link to your website at the end of the post. Avoid dating the post with phrases like "finally Friday" or "have a nice weekend", since you'll be using it as an ad later. Let the post sit on your page for a while to collect some "likes" and comments. Although they aren't important in themselves, from a psychological perspective, people are more likely to read posts that have received more attention through likes and comments. If someone comments on your post, respond with a brief, friendly reply, and remember that others will read it. The more likes and comments you get, the more attractive your post becomes to new customers.

After your post has been on your page for a few days and has gotten some attention, it's time to promote it. Click "Promote", set a budget (e.g., $5 for two days), and choose the target settings for your post (which is now an ad).

Note: If you are just starting and don't have many followers on your page, there is a chance you might not get any likes or comments on your post. It can happen in the beginning. But don't worry, promote it anyway. We all need to start somewhere. Or try sending the post to a few friends who could like and comment to help you get some traction before using it for the ad

4. Ads targeting

All right, let's dive into the technical section. If you're new to social media advertising, it might seem a bit confusing at first. But don't worry; once you start promoting your posts, it'll all start to make sense.

After specifying your target audience in the ad settings, you'll need to select a country (and a city if you offer in-person sessions). Then, you'll be prompted to add an "interest" to target your ad. There's something important to know here: Facebook has recently changed its rules related to the various "interests" we can use in our ads. We used to be able to target almost any spiritual word or term, but many interests (keywords) related to religion, spirituality, and so on have been removed from Facebook. This leaves us with limited options for setting the target interest for a promoted post or ad.

The goal is to find a "keyword" (interest) that captures our ideal customer group (outside the bubble) while still being relevant to the spiritual services we offer. It took me a lot of trial and error to find the right "interest", but looking back, it makes perfect sense. Highly spiritual keywords like "chakra" or "reiki" don't fit our target audience. However, there seems to be one thing that often catches the attention of non- or mildly-spiritual people when they start exploring what we provide: tarot.

When our ideal customer begins searching for spiritual services, they typically encounter tarot cards or readings first. This idea lingers in their minds, and long before they search terms like "medium", "psychic", or "healer", they're likely to explore tarot-related websites or Facebook groups. As they do this, Facebook's algorithm registers these users as "interested in tarot". That's how we find them. So, when you promote your post (as an ad), target women between the ages of 45 and 60 who have an interest in tarot. This way, you'll reach our target audience outside the bubble.

Note: Creating a Facebook ad or promoting a social media post is not complicated; anyone can learn to do it. It may seem intimidating at first, but you'll soon master it. It would likely be confusing to detail this whole process in a text-based format, and challenging to understand by just reading about it. Instead, try searching YouTube for "how to create Facebook ads for beginners" to find helpful tutorials.

5. Patience

When you start creating these posts and ads, not much may happen at first. As we discussed earlier, your future clients want to "get a feel" for you before booking. So, it's crucial to have everything in place: a clear and concise website, an appealing (and not too woo-woo) Facebook page, and all the information and answers your clients might need. Once you've caught their attention, they should be able to go through the whole process themselves, from first contact on Facebook to booking on your website. And this process can take some time, depending on how long you've been in business.

Think about it this way: If you start today, it might take two to three months before you see significant results. You'll receive questions and emails, but bookings could be slow. However, once things start to pick up, they can change quickly. You might go from one booking a week to suddenly having 10-20 bookings weekly. Your customers have simply taken the time to learn more about you and are now ready to book. So don't give up. If you keep pushing forward, bookings and clients will come as long as you've tailored your website and social media to appeal to the right target audience (outside the bubble).

CHAPTER 7
A COMPLETE EXPERIENCE

We've talked about the importance of professionalism, and in this chapter, we're going to dive into creating a "complete experience" for our clients. This means being professional and well prepared at every stage of the process, from the first contact all the way to payment and saying goodbye.

Understanding the Client's Journey

Imagine going to the supermarket and finding, at the checkout, that there are no shopping bags for your groceries (and it happens to be just that day you forgot to bring your own bag..). Suddenly, you've got a problem on your hands. The supermarket might be fantastic with amazing prices, but if customers can't carry their groceries home, it's going to impact their overall experience. Or picture going to the dentist and realizing they don't have a waiting room. You'd have to stand on the street, even in the dead of winter, waiting for your appointment. That's not exactly ideal, is it? While these examples may be extreme, as spiritual practitioners, we need to adopt the same mindset and ensure we're considering the client's experience at every step.

It's common for us, as practitioners, to forget that clients who book spiritual services might feel tense or nervous before their appointment. This is because they don't really know what to expect during a reading or healing session. They're unsure about the information they'll receive and how they'll react to the experience. Will it be emotional? Loving? Or something else entirely? That's why it's crucial to understand the client's journey from start to finish and avoid creating situations that might heighten their tension or nervousness. And always remember who your clients are: people outside the spiritual bubble who may be new to this world.

Where do you meet your clients?

Consider how and where you meet your clients. We'll discuss online consultations via Zoom, Skype, or similar platforms later in the book, but let's focus on in-person meetings for now. When starting a spiritual business, it's common to see clients at home. It's not always workable to rent an office space before gaining momentum in your booking calendar, so home sessions might be the best way initially. However, from the client's perspective, going to a stranger's home can heighten the feelings of uncertainty or nervousness we mentioned earlier. There's a special feeling and energy when entering an unknown person's living space. It's essential to prepare your clients, starting with your website, so they know what to expect. If your website features a cozy image of two armchairs and a small flower by a sunlit window, clients will expect a similar setup during your session.

At the beginning of this book, we mention the stereotype of "an old fortune-teller in a dark basement." Our goal is to move as far away from that image as possible and create an atmosphere that feels normal, pleasant, and not overly mystical. Remember, just because you're a spiritual practitioner doesn't mean your room, where you conduct your sessions, has to scream spirituality. You don't need to hang spiritual decorations or burn sage, and you definitely shouldn't close the curtains or dim the lights. The more "mysterious" the session feels, the fewer clients you'll attract. Existing clients might hesitate to recommend you to their family and friends, which is unfortunate since personal recommendations are one of the best ways to gain new customers. A small number of clients might enjoy a "mysterious experience", but they're often too few and far between to sustain a business. I've attended many readings in my life, and some felt like the haunted house at a carnival—that's not what you should aim for. Strive for a calm, comfortable, and harmonious atmosphere. Of course, if it's winter and dark outside, you can make the space cozy with candles, but keep it welcoming, not mysterious.

When seeing clients at home, remove any personal items that might make them feel uncomfortable or add to the fact that they're in a stranger's house: hideaway bills, vacuum cleaners, dishes, or laundry baskets. Keep the space tidy and clean.

When I first started seeing clients regularly before renting an office, I worked out of our two-room apartment in Stockholm, Sweden. With a small baby at home, our 50-square-meter space was filled with clutter. Before each session, my girlfriend would take our son out, and I'd spend an hour cleaning and preparing for the reading.

Once it was over, I'd call my girlfriend, and they'd return home. It was a huge undertaking, but because I did my best in this situation, I received positive referrals from clients that eventually allowed me to rent an office in Stockholm's old town. If clients hadn't felt comfortable, I'd still be working from that apartment today.

Important information

No matter where you see your clients, they need access to some specific information. Before booking, they should know the price, your address, the date and time of the session, and possible directions to your home or office. They need to know if you record your readings, if they should do so, or if you don't allow it. Inform them about any preparation, like "feel free to bring questions, but keep them to yourself until the end of the reading" or "wear comfortable clothes for your healing session". They should also know about payment options, such as credit cards, cash, or others (we'll discuss this later). Lastly, when clients arrive at your home, they should be able to hang their coats, use the restroom, and have a glass of water if they'd like.

All of this might seem obvious, but missing even one of these details can be like the shopping bag example at the supermarket. If a client needs to use the restroom before a session and there isn't one available, it will impact the entire session and ruin their overall experience. If a client must leave your house, go to an ATM, and return to pay because they didn't receive information about payment options beforehand, it will affect your business. Overlooking minor details can impact the overall experience, which in turn influences whether your clients recommend you to others. Satisfied clients are the best source of new customers. You may give them an exceptional reading or healing session, but if your client is left uncomfortable because they had to hold their jacket in their lap or were thirsty for an hour, they'll leave with an overall negative experience.

Working in the Same Place

One aspect that's more important for you than your clients is establishing a consistent system for each session. Use the same chairs, work in the same room, and create a checklist to remind you to turn off your phone, remove bills from the fridge, or complete any other necessary tasks. By following the same system and making the same preparations every time, you'll streamline the process and find it easier to get into the right energy for your job as a spiritual practitioner. Constantly changing rooms or furniture can affect your performance. You want both you and your client to be as prepared as possible, so you can relax and focus on your job.

A side note: Avoid seeing clients in your bedroom, even if you have comfortable armchairs there. It's too private and can make your client feel uneasy. The same goes if you're traveling, working at a fair, and staying in a hotel. It's common to book additional clients in the evening after working at a fair. If you're already on the road, it's natural to want to take on as much work as possible. However, if you're staying in a hotel, make sure to meet your client and conduct your reading in a more open space, such as a coffee shop or the hotel lounge. Don't bring clients to your hotel room; it can create an uncomfortable atmosphere. I know colleagues who travel a lot and do readings in different countries; they often rent apartments instead of hotel rooms, allowing them to offer a more professional setup and prepare in a kitchen or living room.

CHAPTER 8
MONEY AND PAYMENT

Now it's time to dive deeper into the topic of money and payment connected to our spiritual business. This subject can be sensitive for some, as most practitioners usually don't start their spiritual journey focusing on earning a lot of money. Spiritual practice is often described as a "calling"—an inner spark ignited early in our lives that remains with us throughout our spiritual careers. Many full-time practitioners would agree that if you want to earn a lot of money, there are more lucrative pursuits than working with clients on an hourly basis. However, for most of us, this is something that brings meaning to our lives through helping others, which is why we continue.

If our spiritual practice is our life's path and purpose, then we have the right to make a living from it, charge for our time, and earn an income just like any other profession. Our services are incredibly unique, and despite what some may believe, most of us have invested a lot of time, energy, and resources into honing our spiritual skills. If you ask a medium or healer who's just opened a practice how long they've been doing this, it's not unusual to hear that they've spent 5-10 or even 20 years developing their abilities. Rarely does someone just "decide" one day to become a medium or healer—it's often been a lifelong journey.

MONEY-CHALLENGES

Charging for spiritual services can sometimes come with its own challenges. There are many opinions out there regarding money and pricing, and the source of these opinions can vary. They might come from the public, clients, other practitioners in the industry, or even from within ourselves. Regardless of their origin, these challenges can result in spiritual practitioners feeling like they don't have the right to charge standard rates for their time, and some believe that choosing a spiritual path is to accept a life of low income.

To be clear, the following thoughts are based on my experiences and my perspective on what's appropriate when charging for our services. My hope is that you take on what resonates with you and leave the rest. I've been fortunate enough to work full-time as a medium for many years, and through my work, I've been able to help many people. I take great pride in my work, and I believe my clients appreciate what I do as they continue referring my services to others. In order to devote my life, time, and energy to this path, I've had to adjust my prices to cover costs like rent, salaries, and other expenses. To do this full-time, everything has to add up in the end. Without proper compensation, we can't continue our work. I may not be the cheapest medium, but I'm far from the most expensive. Some colleagues charge two or even three times more than I do, and that's perfectly fine. That's a point many people don't quite understand.

Spiritual services, readings, healing, and everything else within our industry are genuine services. This is our life and reality; those who seek us out do so because they have a real need. A reading or healing session is not a party trick; it is our job. We have families, rent, and bills to pay, just like everyone else, and we have as much right as anyone in any profession to charge forour time. We must acknowledge how unique our services are and how amazing it is that people like us dedicate 20, 30, or even 40 years of our lives to exploring, developing, and practicing our skills. Never apologize for being a spiritual practitioner.

However, we need to adopt a more business-minded approach to make this work. The spiritual energy often keeps us in a state of care and love for our clients, which is vital when working with them. But we must also wear the hat of an entrepreneur and understand that no one benefits if we exhaust ourselves without proper compensation for our time. No one. It's our responsibility to ensure that our work is sustainable, allowing us to have the time and resources to do the job we're meant to do. If that means raising our prices, then so be it, regardless of others' opinions.

Should spirituality be free?

Occasionally, not as much these days, but when I started, I would receive emails from interested clients who had visited my website to book a session. When they saw there was a cost associated with my services (I think I charged $25/hr back then), they would email me and say, "Hi! I'd like to book an appointment with you, but I saw that you charge for your readings. You can't do that as a medium, right? This is a gift you've received for free. You can't charge for it."

To address this "free gift" thing once and for all: The "gift" you've received for free is your "interest" in spirituality and your "desire and drive" to explore and develop your spiritual abilities. However, the courses and workshops, years of practice, setbacks, self-doubt, moments of "should I do this or not", and everything else that comes along with this journey are not free. You've likely, like me, spent several years and a considerable amount of money on courses and various resources to develop your abilities—and that wasn't free. Most spiritual practitioners who work full-time or on a larger scale usually have years of education and training behind them.

To claim that a spiritual practitioner has received their abilities for free is like saying a professional football player has been handed their career for free. While all professional players are born with talent and interest, they have trained nearly every day throughout their careers, and that's what they get paid for. The same applies to us. Everyone has different interests, and those interests are something we all receive for free. However, some choose to develop those interests, and that's what we charge for. I spent about ten years developing my mediumship before I started doing readings, from the first books to attending years-long educational programs. I've taken at least 30 courses and workshops, traveled to various countries multiple times to train, and probably spent $40,000 on mediumship and spiritual development. I've worked hard for a long time to hone my mediumship, and nothing came "for free". I can assure you that I had to work hard to overcome the initial hurdles and stop doubting myself.

LET'S BREAK IT DOWN.

Now that we hopefully agree that it's perfectly acceptable to charge for spiritual services, I thought we would review some of the most critical points concerning money and payment.

1. How much do you need?

The first point is an obvious question, yet many practitioners don't take the time to answer it: "How much do you need to charge for your services?" This is not about "how much others charge", but how much do YOU need to charge for it to work for you? If someone offers reading or healing sessions for $5 an hour as a hobby, that doesn't mean it's the "target price" for that service. Just because someone charges very low prices doesn't mean everyone must do the same. Charging $5 an hour will never create a sustainable business. While some customers might be enticed to "try it" due to the low price, it will never be enough to build a solid foundation for your business.

So, what's your goal, and what would a professional business look like in your eyes? Maybe your own office? Quality services where customers are satisfied with their sessions? Perhaps you'd like to work full-time? You would probably like to earn a reasonable salary to be able to relax and focus on your work. All these things— an office, satisfied customers, and a normal salary — are achievable if you desire. If you want this to be your full-time job, it can be. But you can't build this business if you charge $5-10 an hour. You need to figure out how much you need to charge per hour to make it work for your personal needs.

2. The importance of quality pricing

When I was a teenager, there was a jeans brand called Diesel, which was the newest and hottest thing after Levi's. My friends and I didn't have much money; getting by on a study allowance of $75 a month. Still, we chose to spend nearly the entire amount on a pair of Diesel jeans, even if it meant being broke for the rest of the month. Plenty of other jeans brands cost between $20-30 and were probably just as good. However, we believed Diesel was the best.

Translating this to our services as spiritual practitioners, we can say that our customers— the right customer group outside our spiritual bubble—are ordinary people with jobs and lives like everyone else. They aren't familiar with the significant price differences within our industry; they only see the price you list on your website. If we offer our services for $5 an hour, it appears unprofessional. In an average person's mind, $5 an hour isn't a sustainable price for any service, which can create suspicion about what we do. Going back to the example of a hairdresser: a women's haircut and coloring takes about what, two to three hours? And costs something like $200-300? So how would you feel if you saw a hair salon advertising women's haircuts and coloring for $9.99? It would feel like something was off, right?

The reason a low price can be perceived as unprofessional is because it is unprofessional. I understand that many beginners who want to practice their skills offer their services cheaply, and there's nothing wrong with that. However, you cannot charge beginner rates if you want to grow your business. You must decide how much you want to work, calculate how much you need to earn, and set your prices accordingly.

3. Hours per week

Let's briefly discuss working hours in your spiritual practice (this example is based on working full-time with spiritual services). I don't know any medium or healer who works 40 hours/week with clients only—that would be 40 clients per week. Working as a medium, psychic, or healer requires significant concentration, and concentration consumes energy. As a result, it's challenging to work eight hours a day with clients. When I worked the most, I had about 20-25 private clients, two evening groups, and one weekly stage demonstration. This totaled about 30 hours per week. Nowadays, my business is different, with a large part devoted to students and courses. However, before that, 30 hours was a genuinely busy week. It's important to note that those 30 hours were "paid hours", but I would also spend an additional 15- 20 hours on preparation, travel, administration, websites, social media, etc., that I didn't get paid for.

So, my point is, as a medium, healer, or any other type of spiritual practitioner, you can expect to get paid for about 20-25 hours each week in a typical situation, which should be enough for a full-time functional business. You will still work at least 40 hours/week, as running a business requires much effort, but you won't get paid for 40 hours.

4. It's all about the numbers

I've always run my business by the book, which means I pay taxes on everything I earn. This might seem obvious, but beginner practitioners (in all fields and industries) sometimes overlook this basic legal requirement. How you manage your money is up to you, but if you want a successful business with a salary and pension, you must follow the rules.

A quick side note: I understand that some may not start working full-time immediately. However, the principles we're discussing here are equally important, even if you're doing this as a side job. The goal is the same: to get customers, get compensated for your time, and build a functioning business.

So, let's make a very general calculation (remember, this is just an example based on Swedish tax rates and rules, and it may differ considerably where you live). As a rough guideline, you can assume that out of $100, you'll have $40 left as "your money" (after all taxes). Also, you'll likely only work a maximum of 10 months a year, accounting for periods like summer and holidays when business slows down.

If you charge $50 for a reading or healing session, have 20 clients per week, and work for a total of 10 months, your monthly salary (spread over 12 months) will be about $1,300 after tax. Note that this is with 20 clients per week, 80 clients per month, and 800 clients per year! This is considered a large business in spiritual contexts. Based on this example, you can calculate what is reasonable for you in terms of working hours and prices. If you charge $5 per hour for the same number of sessions (still ten months of work divided into 12 salaries), you'll earn only $130 per month for 80 hours of work. That's unsustainable. On the other hand, if you charge $100 per hour and have your spiritual business as a side job for five hours a week, you'll earn an additional $660 after tax per month.

Again, please remember that this is based on Swedish tax and VAT regulations. These examples are just given to open up your thought process around hourly pricing. Always do your research, follow your country's rules, and consult a professional when in doubt.

5. Comfortable Pricing

This brings us to the next point, which might be on your mind right now: "I can't charge $100 for a session. I don't feel comfortable with that at all." I understand, of course, that it's important for you to feel comfortable with your prices. But I want to emphasize that the "lowest level" that still appears professional and logical to our target audience, those outside the bubble, starts somewhere around $50 per hour (in 2023). Anything below that won't attract more clients, but rather the opposite. You'll lose customers by charging $20 per hour. A price below the accepted "lowest level", in this case $50, unfortunately sends signals that you're not entirely serious or confident in what you do. I know this may sound strange, but for someone seeking, for example, a medium to connect with their deceased father, the contact is so important that they'd rather pay a little more for a medium they perceive as serious than pay less to someone who seems insecure or inexperienced.

And here's the interesting part—if you're new to this industry, your abilities may fluctuate slightly. Some days, things go very well; on other days, you may not get the contact or information you want for your client. It's completely normal, and it can take a while before you develop the routine and experience needed to balance out those slightly "difficult" days. Over time, you'll learn this, and maintaining a consistent level in your readings will become easier. But in the beginning, it can fluctuate a bit. So, set your "real prices" right from the start when you create your website. If you want to charge $50 or $60 per hour, go for it. Then, ensure you never ask for payment in advance, only charging satisfied clients after the session. If you're having a "bad day" and feel like you're not getting the contact you desire, be hundred percent honest with the client: "I'm sorry, but I'm not getting the contact I want today. It's not because of you (the client), but sometimes it's just how it is. It's important to me that you feel you get a good reading, but unfortunately, I don't think I'll be able to deliver that today. So my suggestion is that we end it here. You don't need to pay, of course, and then you're welcome to come back another time or visit another medium if you prefer."

By being honest in this way, you appear professional. You're still working based on the pricing that works for you, but you also know that all the money you earn comes from completely satisfied customers. Over time, you'll have fewer and fewer "bad days", and eventually, everything will go smoothly, and you'll get paid the right amount from the beginning. If you're honest and handle everything professionally, no one will have a problem accepting that you're having a "bad day". However, if you initially set a price of $5 on your website and then want to raise it to $50, it becomes challenging. Such an increase is difficult for your potential customers to accept, which is why you must start with a functional price from the beginning. Then, if you want to raise it from, for example, $60 to $70, it's no problem because you're already above the accepted lowest level, and your followers and potential clients already see you as a professional practitioner.

6. No arguing

When running a professional business and charging real prices, we are also expected to handle clients and situations in a certain way. That's the price WE pay when we charge higher hourly rates. One example of this is that we never argue with our clients. If a client is unsatisfied with their reading or healing session, regardless of the circumstances, they shouldn't pay. And there are no exceptions to this rule. For example, when working with psychic or mediumship readings, clients may book a session expecting to get confirmation of something they think or believe about their lives or others. During the reading, you might pick up on something else that doesn't align with what they want to hear. In this situation, you've done nothing wrong. However, the client might only accept what they're already convinced of, leading them to believe they've received a bad reading, even if it was actually excellent.

Over time, you'll encounter various situations like this. If you find yourself in such a scenario, let it go. Don't start a discussion; accept the client's experience of the reading and allow them to leave without paying. Let go of the situation and prepare for your next client. Forcing an unhappy customer to pay is not recommended, even if you think you're in the right. Trust me on this.

When you have a professional business with professional pricing, it's important to handle unsatisfied customers professionally. Simply let it go. Conflicts can drain your energy in just a few minutes, potentially affecting your performance with other clients that day. If someone is unhappy, let them leave without paying and without any comments or attitude.

7. Payment systems

This last point is about payments and payment systems. To run a professional business, you need to offer your customers and clients convenient payment options. Nowadays, and likely in the future, few people carry a lot of cash in their wallets. Accepting cash can also imply that the money might not be properly accounted for, which we want to avoid. Of course, there will always be clients who prefer to pay in cash, and it's vital that we're prepared to provide a receipt for such payments. As I mentioned earlier, if you set real prices, you're also expected to do the right thing when it comes to reporting your income and taxes.

The best payment options are either card payments connected to a smartphone or iPad (in Sweden, we use Zettle by PayPal, but different countries have different payment systems), which also sends a receipt directly to the customer's email, or using services like Swish (in Sweden), Venmo (in America), or similar services in other countries. It's important for customers to see that they're paying into a business and not a private account. This is something customers are aware of, so if they send a payment to your private account, it's just like making a cash payment; you'll need to provide a receipt.

It's important to repeat: if you charge proper prices, like $50-60 to $100 or more, customers expect you to have a business in the background. If you handle this professionally and smoothly, it will lead to more bookings. If customers feel like you're pocketing $100, it will leave a negative impression, and instead of telling their friends and family about their fantastic experience, they'll feel cheated, and you'll lose customers in the long run. It's simply unfair for someone to earn $300 tax-free a day when the client has worked hard and paid taxes on their money. But, as I said, it's up to each individual and their moral compass. My philosophy is that if you start a business and begin earning extra income, it's essential to follow the rules and do things the right way. If you want your business to grow and continue for many years, you need a stable foundation and accurate financial records.

One last thing: when setting prices, make sure these prices are set "including tax" (or VAT). 99% of your clients are private individuals, and most things they purchase in life include tax (or VAT). When you write a receipt, you can specify the tax amount. If you have a self- employed client who wants to expense the cost through their company, they'll want the tax separately listed on the receipt. It's not difficult or strange. What I often see on websites are various spiritual practitioners listing their prices as "tax not included" or "price + tax." Some might do this to make their prices appear lower than they are, but for a private person who isn't familiar with this, it looks messy and unprofessional. If you charge $70 for a healing session, that's the price you put on your website. If you then have to pay tax on that amount, it's not something the customer needs to worry about. I often see courses and workshops online with prices listed without tax, which doesn't look good. For private clients, it looks complicated, and I'm convinced it leads to losing customers in the long run. Clients want to know exactly what something costs and what they'll pay, and they shouldn't have to calculate the final price themselves.

CHAPTER 9
AUTOMATE YOUR BUSINESS

In this chapter, we'll discuss how to "automate" certain aspects of our business. If you haven't done this before, it might feel like a new concept, but it's not as complicated as it seems. Automating is important if you want to work on a larger scale as a medium, psychic, healer, or in any other spiritual practice. So, what we do when automating our business is examine all the tasks that aren't directly related to our work with sessions and clients, the "unpaid time." We also look at the tasks we repeatedly do and figure out how to avoid doing the same thing over and over.

As we've mentioned throughout this book, running a spiritual business is about finding a system and method to consistently attract new clients to our booking calendar. When we automate parts of our business, we ensure that the entire process, from the first contact (e.g., someone seeing your name on Facebook) to a scheduled appointment, takes care of itself. This may sound impersonal, but once you apply what you learn in this book, you might find yourself suddenly spending a lot of time in front of your computer, communicating with potential clients.

As people become interested in you and your business, they'll have questions and want answers before booking an appointment. If you only receive one email with a question, it's easy to send a personal reply. But if you get 30-40 emails a week with the same questions, you'll quickly realize you're spending a lot of time writing the same answers. Automating your business isn't about being impersonal; it's about staying ahead and addressing all the questions before your clients ask them.

From a sales perspective, whenever a new customer or client needs an answer to a question to proceed in the booking process, you risk losing them as a customer. Importantly, this isn't about "tricking" or "snaring" new customers; it's about having a professional system that allows customers to go through the entire process, from your Facebook post to the booking calendar, without having to stop and email you a bunch of questions. So, when we automate, we look at the entire process and ask ourselves, "What types of questions do I often receive via email, and at what point in this process does the client need to contact me to move forward?"

For example, on my Swedish course page (Mediumkurser.se), there's a link in the menu labeled "Archive". If you click on it, you'll find several blog posts and videos where I provide detailed answers to questions I've repeatedly received over the years. Instead of writing these answers every time I receive an email, I can refer interested customers to the "Archive". This doesn't mean that I'm impersonal in my contact with my clients or customers—quite the opposite. Instead of answering with a "summary email", I give clients access to a professional and solid resource. My potential clients can watch videos and read answers to frequently asked questions. We don't need to email back and forth, and I don't need to write the same email repeatedly. So, this is an example of "automating" your business. When I don't have to spend all day answering emails, I can focus on what's most important—working with clients and building a functioning business. Now, this example is based on my website for online courses, but the same idea applies to all types of websites.

IDENTIFYING THE ROADBLOCKS

In your current business or the business you plan to start, where can you imagine customers getting stuck, leaving, and searching for another medium or healer? Generally, you can say that any point where your customer or potential client needs to contact you to get an answer represents a "roadblock" that could lead to losing bookings. If we examine our customers' journey through the booking process, we can identify and handle potential roadblocks before they become problematic.

So, the first step is usually a post or an ad on, for example, Facebook. If that post doesn't have a link to your website, you've already lost most of those who were interested in what you wrote about in the post. Very few customers will take the time to search for you on Google. The next step is on the website. If clients have to contact you to ask about your services or prices, they may back out. The final step is "booking". If your customers have to email back and forth to find a time that suits both of you, this will also significantly impact your business.

As you can see from this simple breakdown, it doesn't take much before our potential customers decide to move on to another practitioner. When your customers see your post or ad on Facebook and think, "Wow, this sounds exciting; I want to know more", they shouldn't have to send three emails before getting answers to their questions. Everything should be ready beforehand, and even if you're at home sleeping, a customer should be able to go through the entire process and book a session without you having to do anything. This is what I mean by automating your business.

WHEN OUR SYSTEM WORKS

When everything is in place, it should look like this: A customer sees your post on Facebook and clicks the link, which takes them to your website's homepage (landing page), where they see your name and picture. From there, they click on "services" or "sessions" and read about what you offer. Under this description, they can also clearly see the price and length of the session. Then, they can click on a small button that says something like "Book Now", which is linked to your online booking calendar (many apps and companies online offer this booking service). They book their reading or healing session and automatically receive a confirmation email (which you've set up in the booking system beforehand). The confirmation email contains all essential information: time, location, date, payment options, and everything else they need to know. At the bottom of the confirmation email (and this is handled by the booking system, so it's nothing you need to fix), the system will automatically have instructions for "rescheduling" or "canceling", so your client can reschedule or cancel their appointment themselves.

Here we have the entire process, but there's still a chance that questions may arise. In such cases, they'll likely come before the customer clicks "book now" on your website. So on your website, you have a tab called "contact", and it's great to have a ready-made contact form there for them to fill in their email address and message. Additionally, on the contact page, you should include an FAQ (frequently asked questions) section where you answer all the common questions you've repeatedly received via email. This way, you cover all the information that may not have been included elsewhere on the website. Now you're covered! Now you're "automated". You can focus on working with clients, and all you need to do besides that is be active on Facebook. Everything else, the entire process in between, takes care of itself. If you go on vacation for two weeks, the business doesn't need to stop. You simply block off the two weeks on the booking calendar, and when you return, you'll have new clients who have booked ahead, and you can start working immediately.

Only work when you work

While we're on the subject of bookings, calendars, and working hours, there are two more things we need to address: The first is "only work when you work". Stick to the times and dates you've set up in the booking calendar, and say no to requests outside of these. Always refer to the booking calendar on your website. This is the professional way to work; your clients will respect and adapt to your schedule.

All forms of spiritual practice require a lot of energy and concentration, which means you'll need time off or a vacation every year. As we mentioned in Chapter 8, you'll likely only be able to book clients for about ten months a year. People usually don't book readings or healing sessions during the holiday seasons, so use these months to rest or go on your own holiday. If you absolutely need to work during this period, then work on something else.

Personally, I'm not great at taking vacations; I like to work, so what I've done over the years is to close down the booking calendar during certain periods and simply work on something else during that time, such as creating courses, writing books, podcasts, or something completely different.

The second thing is: don't forget to separate your spiritual practice from your personal life. As spiritual practitioners, we work with something that is extremely close to ourselves and our personality. If we take the example of mediumship, this is often something we "are", not something we "do". Mediumship is a part of our life and identity, which makes it challenging to put it aside when we're done working for the day. I'm not talking about this from an energy perspective now; I'm not talking about being "open or closed"—that is, of course, something important to keep track of. What I'm talking about is separating work from personal life.

When you've finished your scheduled bookings and clients for the day, that's it. You need to create a clear boundary between your personal and professional lives, which means not giving out personal information or phone numbers and not answering calls for readings in the middle of the night. This might seem obvious, but many spiritual practitioners feel a sense of duty to everyone who seeks their help. However, if you don't establish these boundaries, you risk burning out and being unable to continue your practice. A common pitfall is feeling a sense of obligation or guilt toward clients who are extremely eager to get help immediately. But an overly eager client may not be in the best position to truly absorb the information or healing you have to offer. This intense eagerness often stems from a belief or thought that they want you to confirm, and they may not be receptive to other insights you provide. So instead, please direct them to your booking calendar, which gives you a buffer of time before the session takes place. This allows the client to potentially calm down, or, as is often the case, they may not book at all. That's perfectly okay. Working with clients who don't have an open mind can be unproductive, so it's better to let those bookings go.

CHAPTER 10
THINKING OUTSIDE THE BOX

In this chapter, we'll explore creative ways to offer spiritual services that cater to a wider audience and increase your income beyond private sessions. Many potential clients are intrigued by the services we offer, but not all of them are ready for the depth and intimacy of a private session or reading. These clients may have limited experience with the type of services we offer and may prefer to ease into it gradually before committing to a private session.

One popular example I've worked with for years is "group readings". In a group reading, I visit the client's home, where they've invited friends, and I give a small mediumship demonstration for the group, which typically consists of 5 to 10 people. The demonstration lasts an hour, followed by a 30-45 minute Q&A session. This allows clients who aren't ready for a private session to experience it together with friends in a comfortable setting. From a business perspective, I can work with more clients in a shorter time frame. Although each participant pays less than they would for a private session, offering group readings is more economically profitable overall.

The idea here is to explore various ways to offer our services to reach more people. Keep in mind that this is a delicate balance. We can offer our services in different forms, but we must also stay within the boundaries of what's accepted in our industry. If we make it unclear, too woo-woo, or create strange names for our services, they won't be successful. As we've discussed before, it's essential to consider the right customer group—clients outside our spiritual bubble.

Now, let's look at some common alternatives to private sessions. Most of these ideas are well-established and probably familiar, but I'd like to explore them to spark your imagination and encourage you to think of new possibilities or unique variations of these popular services. As a disclaimer, my background is in mediumship, so I'll examine these options from that perspective. However, no matter your specialization—medium, psychic, healer, etc—you can adapt these ideas to fit your offerings. For instance, I believe the field of healing has great potential for development and innovation in various exciting ways.

SERVICES

In the early stages of your business, when you're building the foundation for a full-time career, private sessions will likely be your primary product. These sessions create ripples, leading clients to recommend you to friends and family. A private session is just that—a session—and, from the perspective of the clients expectations, there isn't much room to experiment here. However, you can differentiate between a "psychic" and a "mediumship reading" (different mediums use various terms to describe these services). In my case, a psychic reading focuses on the client's energy, touching on their past, present, and potential future. These readings cater to clients with many questions or those facing life decisions. In contrast, a mediumship reading focuses on contact with a friend or loved one who has passed away. Although there's some overlap between the two services, as mediumship is always involved, the focus of the reading is directed to better meet the client's needs.

For instance, if you primarily work with cards, such as tarot or angel cards, and do these types of readings, be clear about that. Tarot and card readings are well-established services in our industry, and many clients are specifically looking for them. Many find the visual aspect of card readings exciting, so if you enjoy working with cards, consider marketing it specifically as a "card reading" rather than just a "reading".

So, here you have three different services to offer: psychic readings, mediumship readings, and card readings. As a medium, you can offer all these services on your website, which doesn't change much for you as a practitioner but rather makes it easier for clients to find an appealing option. All of these services are still private readings, and you simply adjust your focus to meet the client's needs.

GROUPS

The next option is working with groups, which is both fun and economically beneficial for your business. If you're a new practitioner and have just started your business, you might not work with groups immediately. However, it's worth noting that once you begin offering private readings, you'll likely receive inquiries about group events. Clients who have had a positive private reading experience with you may want to book you for an evening event and share this experience with family or friends.

When working with groups, you can customize the event to suit your style of work. Generally, if a group consists of more than 20 people, it becomes challenging to maintain the same level of contact with everyone, turning the event into more of a mediumship demonstration. For home visits or smaller gatherings, you should aim for fewer attendees to create a more "exclusive" atmosphere. While it's essential to tell them that not everyone may receive a message, with smaller groups, there is a higher likelihood that most participants get some type of contact. Some may receive more information than others, depending on their life circumstances and the urgency of their loved ones on the other side. Nevertheless, all participants can appreciate the group reading experience, even if they don't receive direct contact.

This is how I work with groups, but of course, there are many exciting variations: group readings, home visits with individual sessions (everyone gets a private 20-minute reading), or a morning workshop at the client's home that concludes with a small demonstration. You can come up with whatever you want. Another type of home visit could involve house and energy cleansings for mediums who specialize in that.

So here we also have four to five alternative services we can offer our clients to reach more customers. In my experience, all forms of group sessions are quite popular. I often receive emails afterward from the person who booked the session, telling me how exciting they thought it was and how their friends spent hours discussing the experience afterward. Of course, it's great for your business to capture ten satisfied customers in two hours, as it creates ripples and leads to more bookings for private readings.

Demonstrations (Séances)

The next option we have is large-scale séances or mediumship stage demonstrations, which are just two different names for the same thing (in Sweden, we say "big séance", and in England, they say "demonstration of mediumship"). Here, we work with larger groups, ranging from 20 to 30 people up to several hundred.

A side note: All these different services—private sessions, groups, or demonstrations— can certainly be adapted for healers or other spiritual practitioners. People are interested in what we do, and I'm convinced that it's possible to adapt different forms of practice for larger audiences. I even think that, with a bit of creativity, you could probably hold a tarot demonstration for 100 people. Using today's technology, you could have a small camera aimed at the cards and a projector on the wall. It would definitely work and be very exciting if you had a good pace and did shorter readings for members of the audience. This is just an idea, but it's a great example of thinking outside the box while staying within the boundaries of what's accepted and established in the industry.

From a business perspective, large demonstrations can vary in terms of profit. There are two common variants: one is when you're invited to hold a demonstration, for example, at a spiritual association or similar organization. This association, being its own business, often covers much of its expenses, such as rent and other costs, through income from its visitors. The ticket revenue goes to the association, and you, as a medium, may be offered a symbolic amount for your work or asked if you would consider doing it for free. This is an excellent platform for reaching new customers and gaining more experience working with demonstrations and large groups. These events are often very pleasant, and it doesn't matter if you don't receive any compensation. They can often cover your travel expenses and always provide refreshments before or after your demonstration. You can view these events as "marketing", as during the one and a half hours you work, you have the opportunity to showcase yourself to maybe 50-100 people who, in the coming weeks, could generate 10-20 new bookings for private sessions. It's also good to support these associations, as their work helps spread knowledge and interest in what we do. In the end, everyone benefits.

The second option is to organize your own demonstrations. Once you've been in the business for a while and have established your name and "brand" as a spiritual practitioner, this is something worth considering. Basically, you rent a space (often from the same spiritual association we mentioned earlier), but the difference is that you handle everything yourself. You market your demonstration, set up the venue, manage tickets and payments, provide refreshments, and ultimately keep the profits. Of course, this requires having an audience and being somewhat established, but many mediums exclusively travel (even internationally) and make a living doing demonstrations.

These larger performances can really open up opportunities to think creatively. I've been to many demonstrations where mediums have worked with a variety of techniques, such as ordinary mediumship, incorporating flowers, singing, painting, or something similar. Instead of using tarot cards, for example, they might paint a picture on stage, link it to someone in the audience, and do a reading. It may sound abstract, but it actually works. The key is to stay within the audience's expectations (in this case, some form of mediumship) while experimenting with new and exciting elements. One great example I've seen was a medium who drew everything on a large whiteboard, transferring his clairvoyant images and engaging the audience. It worked wonderfully.

COURSES

Another way to expand your business is through circles, workshops, courses, or private lessons. To do this, you first need to establish a solid foundation and have a lot of experience with private sessions before working with students. I usually say, "When it's time, you will know." After a few years of private sessions, clients may start requesting your help in developing their own abilities. And then, if it feels right, go for it.

When speaking about courses, there are countless creative variations. Options range from weekly spiritual circles and weekend workshops to private lessons or year-long online and offline courses. Find what feels right for you, determine how you want to work with students, and decide how big a part of your business this should be. Keep in mind that working with students can be time-consuming and energy-intensive, especially for longer trainings and courses. I used to work with private students in one-hour sessions. Once the session was over, my job was done. Nowadays, I have my online students for two years, which means I need to be engaged and answer questions seven days a week. I've tried various course formats, and I enjoy this approach. It works for me, and I don't mind doing it every day.

Just like everything we've discussed so far, you can tailor your services to fit your style and make them appealing to your clients, but remember to stay within the boundaries of what's expected. Another crucial point is that courses or workshops are marketed to customers and clients "inside the bubble"! Courses and workshops don't have the same target customer group as private sessions. So, when we market our services on platforms like Facebook, we must target the right audience with our offers. Private sessions or healing sessions are aimed at the target group outside the bubble: usually women between the ages of 45 and 60 with moderate or no spiritual interest. When we market our courses, we target people with an existing interest—those within the bubble. The age group within the bubble is roughly the same, but these customers are easier to find. They're in all those spiritual Facebook groups, so you can market directly to the right customers. For bigger demonstrations, our customers fall somewhere between these two groups. I'd suggest marketing a demonstration to people "within the bubble" because they'll likely bring their friends who are "outside the bubble". I hope this makes sense. Depending on where they are on their spiritual journey, people are interested in different services. During a private session, we "sell" information that appeals to those outside the bubble. During a course, we sell "spirituality", which appeals to those within the bubble. And during a demonstration, we sell an "experience" that can appeal to both customer groups.

Fairs and events

The final option for reaching more customers is through fairs and various events. When I say the final option, I don't mean there aren't any other ways to reach out. Instead, under the "Fairs & Events" category, we can include everything else we might come up with as spiritual practitioners. If it's not a private session, a demonstration, a course, or a fair, we can call it an "event". A spiritual trip to Peru with a hike to Machu Picchu could be considered an event.

Fairs

So, a fair is a fair, and an event is everything else. But if we start with fairs, I've learned some important lessons here. In recent years, spiritual fairs have surged in popularity, and there are now many to choose from. They range from large, established fairs with thousands of visitors to smaller, local fairs at spiritual centers nationwide. Similar local spiritual fairs also exist in neighboring countries. For example, I've worked at fairs in Denmark that closely resemble those in Sweden, with many of the same exhibitors.

When it comes to fairs, they're a great way to get noticed and market yourself. From an economic perspective, they usually offer the chance to earn some extra money, as you can see many clients for short sessions in just a few days. And here's a little tip that's particularly important when working at larger fairs: instead of trying to do as many sessions as possible, take longer breaks between sessions to chat with visitors. I recall a large fair I attended in Stockholm, where I scheduled three readings per hour throughout the event. Financially, it was rewarding, but I was fully booked and occupied, leaving no time to engage with the visitors standing next to my booth.

After the fair, I had the earnings from my readings but hadn't managed to generate much interest from other visitors. So, the next time, I planned for one 20-minute reading per hour and dedicated the remaining 40 minutes to conversations with visitors. This approach led to better financial gains through private bookings in my regular calendar. By not being overly busy with three clients per hour, I could talk to 10 potential customers per hour, which is more profitable in the long run.

When it comes to smaller, local fairs, this isn't as important. At a smaller fair, there are fewer visitors, and there are usually natural gaps during the day for talking to people. Generally speaking, the goal of a fair should be to generate interest among potential new customers rather than trying to make as much money as possible in a short time. $500 earned at a fair could translate into $3,000 in your regular booking calendar if you take the time to talk to visitors and give them your contact and website information.

Events

As for events, they can be anything you like: a trip abroad, a spiritual walk in the woods, a day of channeled writing, or whatever else you can think of. You can be pretty creative with this, but as with everything, stay within the boundaries of what's expected and established. If you come up with an event, it should be connected to something the participants are familiar with, like a try-out healing day or a forest walk to open your mediumistic senses (I'm just making this up, but you get the idea). If it's called "a spiritual night at the farm", then customers might not really know what to expect. "Are we going to develop spiritually, or is it some kind of haunted house experience?" When there are too many questions, customers will hesitate. Be clear about everything you do and target the right customer group.

Two more things

Before we wrap up this chapter, I want to mention two more things. First, if you have an idea, just go for it. Sometimes it works, and sometimes it doesn't, but that's okay. Taking chances is part of finding your own way of working. If you're new to the field of spiritual practice and have taken a course with others, consider creating an event or doing a demonstration together to take the pressure off a bit. Just ensure you stay active and always charge for your time when working with clients, regardless of the service or event you offer.

Second, when you've been a spiritual practitioner for a while, it's common to discover a few preferred ways of working. Instead of doing everything simultaneously, try switching between them during different periods. For example, you might focus on private sessions for awhile, and then, if you have many students and courses, you could close your booking calendar for a period (assuming the courses and students can sustain your income). Sometimes, doing too many things at once can leave you feeling scattered. So, if you've established your business in multiple areas, consider shifting your focus during different periods to add variety to your everyday work.

CHAPTER 11
WORKING ONLINE

In this chapter, we're going to discuss working online and explore the opportunities available for spiritual practitioners to offer their services over the Internet. When it comes to working online, there are two key aspects to consider: the types of services we offer that work well online, and the tools or platforms we use to communicate with clients or sell products and services online.

SERVICES

First, let's take a look at what services might work online. Keep in mind that, just as we discussed in Chapter 10, there are numerous creative ways to offer services online. As technology continues to develop, it will become even easier to expand our offers. Currently, some of the most common and established online services are private sessions, such as various types of readings where you speak with the client "live" in real-time over the Internet. Although I haven't seen this as much in healing practices, I can imagine that "distance healing" might involve a meeting online before or after the session to follow up with the client.

Another popular service, as mentioned earlier, is online courses, which have exploded in popularity over the last couple of years. With online courses, we can reach a much larger audience since there are no geographic limitations. We can theoretically have students from around the world and are not constrained by specific dates and times for individual lessons. We can pre-record our lessons, and students can complete the course at their own pace.

And finally, not a "service", but physical or digital products that we sell via our website as either downloadable items or physical products that we ship out.

PROS AND CONS

Let's first take a look at online sessions or readings, which are established and accepted services among our customer group. A few years ago, some practitioners were skeptical about conducting sessions over the Internet, but today it's proven to work perfectly fine. Many practitioners have been working over the phone for years, so using platforms like Zoom, Skype, or other similar options works great. For example, in my online courses, students complete at least 20 readings and eight hours of practice with clients—all done online without any issues.

The advantages of offering readings over Zoom, for example, include reaching a larger customer base, not needing to rent a physical space or having to tidy up your home for clients, and also having the flexibility to work while traveling or on vacation.

On the other hand, the disadvantages of conducting online sessions can be the initial setup or technology surrounding the session, which might be somewhat distracting if you're not used to it. If you don't feel confident and comfortable with the technical aspects, relaxing before starting the session can be difficult.

The second disadvantage is that if the session becomes highly emotional, you're not physically there to support the client in the same way as you would in person. Of course, it's easier to be present for the client when you're in the same room, especially when emotions run high. You can handle this online by talking to the client, but it might be challenging if you're not used to doing it.

The third disadvantage is payment. As I've mentioned before, I always recommend not taking payment in advance when working with clients. Instead, only accept payment after a session when you know the client is satisfied. This can be a bit tricky when working online, as you can't be entirely sure that you'll get paid. I say this because I've experienced this several times. It's not a massive problem, but customers who claim to be very satisfied occasionally choose not to pay for their session. Another challenge is that sometimes clients miss their appointments due to technical issues or simply don't respond when you try to contact them, leaving you with a booking and an hour for which you don't get paid. In these situations, I recommend returning to my "no arguing" philosophy that I mentioned earlier: simply accept the loss and let it go. I don't make a big deal out of these things, and I've never tried to "collect" a missed payment. In the long run, it's better for you and your business if you just let it go and instead focus on the next client.

So, if I had to pinpoint the biggest challenge or hurdle to working with clients and conducting sessions online, it would be gaining enough experience in this area to "tune out" the technical aspects and focus entirely on your job.

Even if you have a good computer and a good webcam, there's no guarantee that your client has the same, and you may have to work looking at a blurry or lagging image during the session. That's okay; it shouldn't hinder your work. With time and experience, you'll learn how to work effectively in this online environment.

ONLINE COURSES

The second type of service we mentioned was online courses. With these, we also have the opportunity to reach a wide range of people geographically, and students can purchase a course and complete it at their own pace. For spiritual and mediumship development courses, it's not uncommon for customers to have different preferences, with many still opting for in-person courses. One reason for this is that people enjoy being part of a group when learning something new, offering each other support. However, online courses are becoming increasingly popular, and by having the enrollment "open and close" at specific times during the year, you can create a sense of community as students feel they are taking the course alongside others. By doing it this way, no one feels they are the "lone new beginner".

Another aspect of online courses is that, if done right, they can become "evergreen products", meaning that you create the course once and then sell it repeatedly for several years. This might sound like a dream come true—as if you'll never have to work again. However, that's not the case. If you enjoy teaching courses and feel comfortable with all the technology and everything related to working online, creating online courses can be an excellent option. But don't be fooled into thinking it's a quick and easy project that will effortlessly generate a lot of money. From my own experience, creating online courses can be a time-consuming process. Take the first online course I created, for example; it required six months of planning and preparation, followed by two months of recording, editing, and setting up the online course portal. On top of that, it's not unusual for me to spend seven days a week answering emails and questions from my students.

Now, I don't say this to discourage anyone, but I happen to be quite familiar with the technology involved in creating online content, courses, and products. I attended film school when I was younger and have worked on numerous film projects, so I'm well-versed in computers, cameras, lighting, and sound. Of course, you don't have to make your courses so advanced; you could even create them using your smartphone. However, if you're new to creating digital products or courses, a learning curve may be involved.

I believe anyone who offers in-person courses should consider whether they can be adapted into online products. This can add value to your business, but it's important not to rush the process or produce poorly thought-out content. If you want to sell a high-quality, "evergreen" product for years to come, it's crucial to get it right from the beginning.

Physical or Digital Products

As for physical or digital products, there are many possibilities, including books, e-books, meditations, tarot cards, and more. These can be evergreen products that you create once and sell indefinitely. For instance, if you enjoy writing, a downloadable e-book could provide additional income through your website. Guided meditations are also popular and well-suited for online sales. However, I want to emphasize that you shouldn't create a product "just because". A hastily made digital product could reflect poorly on your entire business. By taking your time and ensuring you produce a high-quality product, you'll likely attract more customers and fill up your booking calendar.

To get some ideas about these products, visit your favorite spiritual practitioner's website and see what they offer. They also usually have what's called a "lead magnet" (a downloadable product you get for signing up for their newsletter), and this type of lead magnet is a great thing to create and offer on your website to get people to sign up for your email list. Then, in the future, you can market your courses, services, and products to this email list with the knowledge that the people receiving these emails are already familiar with and interested in your business.

The importance of quality

I highly recommend expanding your business by offering services, courses, and online products. When done well, they can positively impact your bottom line. But remember not to rush the process. For example, when it comes to courses, books, and e-books, people expect a certain level of quality, format, and structure. If you take shortcuts, you may end up with a subpar product that fails to meet your audience's expectations.

I might come across as slightly negative about this topic, making it out to be a difficult thing, but that's not my intention at all. I'm a firm believer in building and establishing your business online. What I mean is that our online presence should maintain the same level of quality as our offline physical business. What many people consider "easy and obvious" regarding online services actually requires more time, energy, and preparation than one might initially think. With that said, if you recognize and accept that your online offers reflect your offline business, you can create products and services that benefit your business both financially and in terms of marketing. Working online is just as demanding as working offline. The time spent writing a book or creating a course could have been used for client sessions. It's essential to consider this trade-off. Just like when launching a new website, customers will want to explore your online presence and get a feel for your products before making a purchase. This means it may take some time before a course or downloadable product generates revenue.

First step online

When starting online, the first step is typically offering private, hourly sessions. This is the service you'll want to establish and make work before tackling anything else. Online sessions help build the financial foundation we discussed earlier. These sessions should be conducted similarly to regular, offline sessions. Meaning, the spiritual service you offer, such as healing, psychic, or mediumship readings, should be provided in the same way. Once you're comfortable with the technical aspects, the process becomes much easier.

One critical point we've emphasized in this book is addressing potential questions or concerns from customers or clients. Just as we discussed, being transparent on your website about what happens before, during, and after a reading or session and providing extra clarity for online services is vital. While you may be familiar with different online communication tools, your clients might not be, which can create uncertainty and lead to potential clients backing out. Currently, the most common tools for online sessions are Zoom and Skype (though this may change over time). By "most common", I mean that these are the programs that our specific target audience is most familiar with. While there are other options like Messenger or various platforms available, Zoom and Skype remain the most recognized choices (as of 2023). It's best not to overwhelm your website visitors with too many options. Instead, decide on one or two platforms, like Zoom and Skype, and provide a link for customers to download the programs if they don't already have them installed on their computers.

Always explain the process to your clients. For example, "I'll call you on Skype at your scheduled time. Please make sure you're in a quiet environment and, if possible, wear headphones or a headset." Then, when the session starts, let the client know they can click the small recording button if they want to record the reading, or inform them if recording isn't allowed. Another essential tip for conducting online readings is to give yourself some time before and after each session. Despite being well prepared, technical issues can arise, so it's helpful to have a few extra minutes to ensure the camera and sound are functioning correctly.

The big picture

Now let's step back and consider the bigger picture of working online. It's not inherently more difficult or easier than other methods. Once you're familiar with the technology and get into the routine of meeting clients online, it can be a relaxed and enjoyable way to work. Online services offer new opportunities for your business, most notably access to a larger customer base. If you speak English well, you can cater to clients from around the world. For example, I'm Swedish but often receive inquiries from English-speaking clients.

Online services and products will become even more popular in the future. Even if you primarily see clients in person today, this trend will likely change, and customers will eventually expect us to offer our services online. So, if you can and want to, it's a good idea to explore online possibilities sooner rather than later. Consider how you might adapt your current spiritual circles, workshops, or courses to suit an online audience.

It's true that online interactions can create a slight distance between you and your clients, a distance that doesn't exist in face-to-face meetings. However, we can't ignore the fact that our society is increasingly moving online. Everything from groceries and books to professional services is now available on the Internet, and our services are no exception. Rather than viewing this trend negatively, we should embrace it and capitalize on the available opportunities.

Working online offers both you and your clients the freedom to work and access services whenever and wherever you want. More and more people value this convenience. Even if you're not ready to develop your online business right now, keep the idea in mind. It might be the opportunity that transforms your entire business and allows you to work full-time as a spiritual practitioner.

CHAPTER 12
ENTREPRENEURSHIP

At this point, we've covered most of the key aspects of running a spiritual business, and by now, you should have an understanding of how to attract and work with clients. I know it might seem overwhelming at times, especially when it comes to target audiences, websites, and marketing. However, it's not as complex as it appears. As long as you grasp the idea of clients who are "in the bubble" and those who are "outside the bubble", you can make this work. Throughout this book, I've mentioned that our work as spiritual practitioners is special and unique, but our goal shouldn't be to make it "more special" or "more unique". Instead, we should strive to make our services feel as "normal" as possible. When clients see our services as exciting, approachable, and welcoming, we can build full-time careers just like any other profession.

Another thing we have touched on is the technical and administrative aspects of starting and running a business, and I thought we should take that subject for another spin. While we won't delve too deeply into the technical side, we will discuss it more broadly, focusing on how we can be perceived as professional practitioners and the image we present to our clients regarding ourselves and our industry.

If you're already running a spiritual business, you're likely familiar with the importance of keeping track of receipts, invoices, and taxes, either on your own or with the help of an accountant. You know that managing finances can be tricky, and it may take some time to learn what you can handle yourself and what requires assistance. The main difference, if you are already doing it, is that you've already crossed that "starting a business" threshold. You're in the "mindset", understanding that you are responsible for making everything work. While some people are natural entrepreneurs who enjoy this aspect, others may not. However, it's essential not to let this part overwhelm our spiritual practice. Our focus should remain on our services— readings, healing, or whatever we offer—and everything else should run smoothly in the background.

For those new to entrepreneurship, starting and running a business can seem daunting. Working with clients might feel familiar and safe, but the idea of managing a business can be intimidating for many. It doesn't have to be as scary as you think, though. You can start a small, one-person operation as a sole proprietorship or LLC and open a bank account to deposit a certain percentage of your weekly earnings, which will be used to pay taxes. With an accountant handling receipts and taxes, you can then receive your final earnings as a salary. It doesn't have to be more complicated than that.

WHY DOES THIS MATTER?

You might wonder, "Why is all this technical business stuff so important?" The short answer: it's the law. As a business owner, you're required to pay taxes, and not doing so is illegal. While I personally don't focus on how others earn or report their money, I believe that the energy we work with as spiritual practitioners is reflected in the energy we surround ourselves with. Running an honest, loving business positively impacts our work, while cheating and prioritizing personal gain negatively affect it, as clients can intuitively sense the energy.

I'm not here to preach morality; I only take responsibility for my own business. However, I'm confident that if spirituality and your spiritual practice bring meaning to your life and you feel it's your path and destiny, you'll naturally want to do more of it. To be able to build up a client base and devote time to your spiritual business, you must charge for your services and earn an income like any other job. You should be able to get a mobile phone subscription, rent an apartment, or save for retirement, just like everyone else. This isn't possible if you don't handle your money correctly.

Even if you have another job and income, it's wise to establish your spiritual business properly from the start. This allows you to easily evaluate if you want to quit your other job and pursue spiritual work full-time. With clear financial records, you'll know how many readings you need monthly to earn a salary. It may take time to build up your business or make the transition, but knowing you've created a functional business alongside your regular job that generates a certain amount each month is empowering. If circumstances change or you feel ready, you can expand your business and become a full-time spiritual practitioner when the time is right.

Being Professional

The crux of spiritual entrepreneurship is understanding that we're already in an industry where clients might view us with skepticism. Historically, there have been many questions surrounding what we do, and the only way to build sustainable careers is by being 100% professional. By doing everything the right way from the start, we can eliminate these doubts and show our clients that we're serious and professional. This is our job and our reality. While we won't appeal to everyone with our services, those who genuinely need what we offer should be able to book and experience it without feeling cheated or misled. Clients should leave their session feeling like they've had a professional and positive experience, regardless of their beliefs.

Choosing a spiritual career inevitably means facing scrutiny. It's part of the work we do. Clients "outside the bubble" are often unfamiliar with our practices, so they may question themselves. They might experience a conflict between their heart and mind, wanting to contact loved ones on the other side while some other part of them says it can't work. Many spiritual practitioners might bury their heads in the sand when confronted with such doubts, becoming irritated and creating an "us versus them" divide. Don't do that. Embrace the fact that our work is unique and that clients questioning their beliefs might project that onto you, which is okay. As professional practitioners, we understand this and strive to represent our profession in a calm, open and positive way.

If you're uncomfortable with being questioned, you might hesitate to reach out to clients "outside the bubble", preferring to stay within spiritual Facebook groups. But this approach won't bring in new clients or bookings. So accept that an essential aspect of your work, besides the services you offer, involves representing the entire spiritual industry. By doing so in an open, friendly, and professional manner, you'll ultimately benefit all of us.

CHAPTER 13
NEXT STEP

Now it's time to summarize this book and emphasize the crucial step of putting what you've learned into action. I want to repeat a point I made earlier: the insights shared in these chapters aren't just my opinions but are based on my experiences from many years of full-time work in this industry. Spiritual business doesn't always work the way we want it to, and we might wish some things were different. But if you embrace the information in this book, you'll start to notice increased interest in your services. So give it a shot, even if it feels uncomfortable, and see what happens. Any unease around spiritual entrepreneurship will fade once your business is up and running.

The key now is to move from knowledge to action, which is something only you can do. When starting something new, it's typical for progress to be slow at first—nothing happens, and you might doubt your decision or think, "It'll never work". However, that's not true. The slow start is simply because nobody knows you yet, and not enough people have visited your website for your booking calendar to start moving. This doesn't mean something is wrong; it just means you need to reach out more actively.

Whether you're just starting out or already have a business with a few clients, don't wait—be proactive, make changes, and ensure things happen. Be willing to explore and experiment. Don't give up until it works. You might find that much of what you've done previously doesn't align with the advice in this book, and that's okay—just be open-minded and dare to do things differently. Remember, when it comes to your brand, you are your brand! The demand for spiritual services grows every year and is becoming more popular. Still, I doubt it'll ever become so mainstream that personal branding becomes irrelevant or healing and mediumship services get marketed under large company names or organizations. Clients will always want to know who YOU are. All sales from your spiritual services will be linked to you as the practitioner. Because of that, it makes sense to market yourself as an individual and use your name as a practitioner. So, instead of names like "Eternal Moon Spiritual Center", eliminate any confusion by simply using your name, such as "Medium Anna Smith". And always remember who your customers are—the people "outside the bubble". Women between the ages of 45 and 60 with moderate spiritual interests who may not be members of spiritual Facebook groups but have the greatest need for your services.

Even if these customers happen to be in one of those Facebook groups, that's not where you'll reach them. Since they know very little about what we do, they tend to be quite reserved in these groups. However, if you reach them outside of these groups, say, through a Facebook ad, they'll be much more interested in booking your services. I know this might sound strange, but it has logic. Picture walking into a gym for the first time in your life, never having exercised before, and having no idea how the machines work. Wouldn't it be better if the gym were empty and quiet so that you could explore it on your own? You wouldn't want to walk in for the first time and find it packed with 100-fit people working out to the max. You'd likely feel lost and out of place. The same concept applies to our target customer group. They might join a spiritual Facebook group, but there's just too much new information to absorb. However, if they can calmly and quietly find your website and read about how everything works, they'll start booking your services.

The Checklist

Before we wrap up this book, I thought I'd provide a helpful resource for you on your journey to building a full-time spiritual business. At the back of this book, you'll find a "checklist" with questions you can ask yourself to assess where you stand in your existing business. Naturally, these questions are related to everything we've covered in this book. The intention is for you to use this list as a simple and comprehensive tool to see which areas work and which changes might help you boost your number of clients and, subsequently, your revenue.

The End

That's it! We've now reached the end of the book, and I truly hope you feel you've gained some valuable and practical knowledge. Whenever I teach something, I always say, "Take what feels good and let go of the rest!" If there was something in this book that didn't resonate with your thoughts or feelings about running a spiritual business, something that felt entirely opposed to your beliefs, that's okay. Embrace what felt right and what you believe will help you grow your business, and let go of what doesn't work for you. The goal is for you to gain clients and customers, build a financial foundation for your business, and get compensated for your time. Anything you do that improves this is a step in the right direction.

Looking at the spiritual industry today, I'm utterly convinced that we've only seen the tip of the iceberg. This field will continue to grow every year, and anyone who's willing and ready to take on the challenge can start and run a successful spiritual business. It's about "getting started" and then changing and improving along the way. If you keep moving forward, things will fall into place, and as they say, "You only regret the things you didn't do". So, make a plan, move forward, and always actively work on developing your business. I wish you the best of luck with everything!

CHECKLIST

Building a Full-time Spiritual Business

Audience and Clarity

- ❑ Target audience: Am I reaching the right customers/clients with my services?
- ❑ Message clarity: Is my message clear, or does it sound too "woo-woo"?
- ❑ Authenticity: Am I open and honest about who I am and what I do?
- ❑ Niche services: Is my business too specialized, offering services that few have heard of?

Website Essentials

- ❑ Name and photo: Are my name and picture clearly visible on my website?
- ❑ Service descriptions: Are my services/sessions clearly outlined on my website?

- ❏ Writing style: Are my website texts friendly and easy to understand?
- ❏ Contact information: Are my email address and contact information easily accessible?
- ❏ Welcoming new clients: Am I sending the right signals to make new clients feel welcome?

Social Media and Marketing

- ❏ Facebook presence: Do I have a business profile on Facebook?
- ❏ Consistent posting: Am I regularly sharing content related to my business?
- ❏ Active promotion: Am I actively marketing myself and my services?
- ❏ Target audience: Am I targeting the right audience with my marketing efforts?
- ❏ Group posting: Do I only share content in spiritual groups?

The Client Experience

- ❏ Client environment: Is my space welcoming and comfortable for clients?
- ❏ Extra touches: Do I go the extra mile to make my clients feel welcome?
- ❏ Complete experience: Am I offering a seamless experience from start to finish?

Money and Payments

- ❏ Pricing: Are my services priced correctly, allowing me to earn a living?
- ❏ Payment options: What payment methods do I offer?
- ❏ Receipts: Can I provide receipts if clients request them?

Automating

- ❏ Redundant tasks: Am I constantly repeating the same tasks?
- ❏ Booking system: Is my booking process efficient?
- ❏ FAQs: Do I have an FAQ section on my website?
- ❏ Business hours: Do I see clients only during working hours?
- ❏ Session types: Do I offer both in-person and online sessions?

Thinking Outside the Box (Diversifying Services)

- ❏ Private sessions
- ❏ Group sessions/home visits
- ❏ Readings/demonstrations
- ❏ Spiritual circles
- ❏ Workshops/courses
- ❏ Private tutoring
- ❏ Fairs/events

Business Growth

- ❏ Professional approach: Am I treating my business as a business?
- ❏ Full-time potential: Can my business grow into a full-time job?
- ❏ Client numbers: Do I know how many clients I need weekly to meet my goals?
- ❏ Future plans: Have I set a roadmap for my business's future?

ABOUT THE AUTHOR

Johan Poulsen is an acclaimed psychic medium, author, lecturer, and teacher. Born in Stockholm, Sweden, Johan's fascination with the spirit world began at a young age. He dedicated much of his time to learning all he could about the mysteries of the spirit world. For the past fourteen years, Johan has worked to share his knowledge and educate others about mediumship and psychic abilities. He helps people change their beliefs and embrace their innate abilities through public appearances, television, and his writing.

Known for his straightforward, no-nonsense approach, Johan has done thousands of private readings, taught mediumship to over a thousand students, participated in interviews, given stage demonstrations, contributed to various magazines, authored the book—*Modern Mediumship: A Complete (Woo-Woo-Free) Course to Become a Successful Psychic Medium*, and starred in the Warner Bros. show, *Swedish Mediums*. Johan lives in the south of Sweden with his family.

www.developmediumship.com

www.ingramcontent.com/pod-product-compliance
Ingram Content Group UK Ltd.
Pitfield, Milton Keynes, MK11 3LW, UK
UKHW022214230426
12048UKWH00016BA/848